Beautifully Scarred

Conquering Clefts, Receiving Adoption, and Embracing Scars

A MEMOIR BY
CAMEY JOY

INVICTUS MANEO
PUBLISHING

Copyright © 2024 by Camey Joy

All rights reserved. No part of this publication may be reproduced, distributed, or transmitted in any form or by any means, including photocopying, recording, or other electronic or mechanical methods, without the prior written permission of the publisher, except in the case of brief quotations embodied in critical reviews and certain other noncommercial uses permitted by copyright law. For permission requests, email the publisher, subject "Attention: Permissions Coordinator," at the address below.

All scripture quotations are from the Holy Bible, New International Version®, NIV® unless otherwise indicated. Copyright © 1973, 1978, 1984, 2011 by Biblica, Inc.™ Used by permission of Zondervan. All rights reserved worldwide.

Scripture quotations marked (MSG) are taken from THE MESSAGE. Copyright © 1993, 1994, 1995, 1996, 2000, 2001, 2002. Used by permission of NavPress Publishing Group.

Scripture quotations marked (AMP) are taken from the Amplified® Bible (AMPC). Copyright © 1954, 1958, 1962, 1964, 1965, 1987 by The Lockman Foundation. Used by permission.

Paperback ISBN: 979-8-9911609-0-2
Hardcover ISBN: 979-8-9911609-1-9
eBook ISBN: 979-8-9911609-2-6

Library of Congress Control Number: 2024921464

Front cover photo by Meshali Mitchell—meshali.co.
Book cover design by Joe Cavazos—joecavazos.com.

Invictus Maneo Publishing, LLC
Austin, TX
inquiries@invictusmaneopublishing.com

First Edition 2024

A Note on Memoir Writing:
Certain liberties were taken with the stories shared in this book. Some of the information presented was gathered secondhand from multiple sources with varying accounts. The dialogue in quotations serves as an approximation, and some conversations have been condensed into one for the sake of brevity. To enhance clarity, events may have been rearranged in chronological order or categorized thematically. In certain cases, individuals present for specific incidents may have been omitted or with name change from the narrative to maintain confidentiality. Please keep this in mind while reading this memoir.

I dedicate this book to my parents,
Rea and Judi Thompson.
Thank you for the gift of adoption.

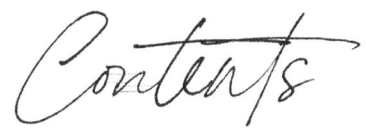

Introduction VII

Preface: Prayer of Gratitude XV

PART I

Chapter One	The Promise	1
Chapter Two	El Milagro (The Miracle)	9
Chapter Three	El Regalo (The Gift)	19
Chapter Four	The Beauty in the Pain	31
Chapter Five	The Call	39
Chapter Six	Not From Around Here	47
Chapter Seven	Finding My Voice	59
Chapter Eight	Resurrecting the Dead	75
Chapter Nine	TKO	85
Chapter Ten	My Extreme Makeover	93
Chapter Eleven	No Mountains in This Valley . . .	115
Chapter Twelve	Wake-Up Call	133

PART II NOTICE:

Due to sensitive content, parental advisory is recommended.

PART II

Chapter Thirteen	Not—Happily Ever After 157
Chapter Fourteen	Warfare 171
Chapter Fifteen	On or Off Stage 195
Chapter Sixteen	Sin Never Stays Hidden 213
Chapter Seventeen	Life After Death 233

PART III

Chapter Eighteen	Dreams 243
Chapter Nineteen	Revealed (Overcoming Scars) . . . 269
Conclusion	The Promise of My Name 281

THE END

Pictures 286

Letter from Nate 289

Letter from Dr. Hobar 291

Acknowledgments 293

About The Author 295

Introduction

It was never my decision to be born with scars. I didn't choose the pain I endured, the rejection I faced, or the overwhelming odds I needed to overcome. With each scar, I tell my story, painfully etched into my skin and my heart, reminding me of moments I never wished for. As I sit here writing and looking back on my life's journey, I reflect on the significance of these scars and how God crafted them to tell a beautiful story to show His goodness, grace, and mercy.

While some people long to erase or hide their scars, I've chosen a different path. I've chosen to embrace my scars, to wear them proudly, for they are a testament to resilience and the battles I've fought. However, this acceptance did not come easily. It required me to acknowledge my wounds and confront my own insecurities, which inspired me to face my fears while truly being honest about how God made me an overcomer, scars and all, even before birth. I've come to understand that each scar has its unique story to tell. They are not just blemishes on my skin but imprints of my experiences—my struggles. Some scars were created out of necessity, while others were formed as the result of daring to be brave, but each one holds a reminder of significant moments in my life and the lessons they taught.

As I survey my scars, I see a map of my life, where each scar represents a memorable chapter in my story. The double scars on my lip remind me of what was once torn apart and is now meticulously sewn together, representing countless medical professionals who never gave up on me. Those scars were the result of a cleft lip and palate, a congenital condition that required extensive corrective surgeries. When I was a newborn, my parents made the brave decision to mend what appeared to most to be an insurmountable divide. Though faint lines today, the scars bear witness to my doctors' unwavering love and the marvel of medical science. The doctors, redirecting a vein from my lower lip to my upper lip, created a bridge of life where there was once a gap. In the 1980s, this was a groundbreaking surgery that allowed me, and many others who followed, to smile without restraint.

Another scar, etched on my left cheek, tells a story of a spirited encounter with an unfriendly animal. It's a smile line, but not the kind that comes from laughter or joy. Instead, this scar took its place as a result of a shocking unexpected dog bite. A momentary lapse in trust between us. In time, the scar has faded, leaving behind a reminder of the unpredictability of life, the fleeting nature of trust, and the power of forgiveness. One of the most prominent scars I bear is one not easily seen, running along the gap inside my mouth as a result of a bilateral cleft palate. Now, when looking at my scars, I see more than just a physical blemish. I see the tapestry of experiences that have shaped me into the woman, the wife, the mother, the daughter, the sister, and the friend that I am today. They are all a reminder of the pain and suffering I've endured.

Two more scars, mostly unseen, linger on my hips. They are like secret markers, a map of sorts, tracing the journey of bone grafts used to repair the roof of my mouth (the cleft palate). These grafts served as the foundation for a strong palate, allowing me to speak and eat with ease.

My physical scars, too numerous to count, are the legacy of countless surgeries, orthodontic treatments, braces, and retainers, each meant to refine my smile and improve my ability to communicate. However, it's the hidden internal scars that are the true wounds of my heart, wounds that are the remnants of past experiences that left emotional imprints on my soul. Scars of shame, moments that caused me to feel small and insignificant; scars of abandonment, scars marking times of isolation and feeling unloved; scars of anger, reactions to life's injustices; and scars of feeling unworthy, a shadow that sometimes looms large and overwhelming. These internal scars are the most enduring because they remind me not only of the hardships I've experienced but also of my resilience, my capacity to heal and grow, and my determination to rewrite the story of my life as God turns my scars into beauty.

DON'T THROW IN THE TOWEL

My parents have always been a constant source of wisdom, and their advice has shaped me in profound ways. I vividly remember a time when they imparted a lesson about a path to healing, a lesson I constantly carry, during a time of immense physical and emotional struggle. I had just undergone back-to-back surgeries, the first of which left my jaws wired shut for a grueling six weeks. I was hoping this was the end of it, that the pain and discomfort I'd endured countless times over would finally be finished. However, this wasn't the case. When my parents informed me that I would need yet another surgery, one that would involve my lips being sewn together for a couple of weeks, I was devastated, disheartened, and utterly exhausted. I wanted to throw in the towel, call it quits, and scream, "I can't do this anymore. I'm done! No more!" Actually, I probably did shout all those things, and it was then that my parents shared their invaluable insight.

They spoke of the necessity of perseverance and the inevitability of pain on the path to healing. They refused to allow me to give up, insisting that I was a person filled with grit and the strength to persevere through even the most challenging trials. They assured me that I would eventually look back on this period of my life and feel grateful that I'd pushed through the pain and adversity. Their consistent support and belief in my resilience became a lifeline during those difficult days. At times, they saw strength I couldn't see in myself. With their encouragement, I resolved to face the upcoming surgery with determination, even though it seemed insurmountable.

Looking back, I am eternally grateful I didn't give up, that I didn't succumb to the overwhelming desire to quit when the going got tough. Those surgeries and the associated pain were excruciating, but they were also transformative. My experience through those surgeries, guided by my parents' wisdom and unyielding support, stillness and faith, there is peace, knowing You are my protector and provider.

"Wonderful are Your works, And my soul knows it very well."

Thank You, God, for blessing me with what I did not know I needed and protecting me from what I thought I wanted. Your wisdom surpasses my own, and I'm grateful for Your divine discernment. You've given me gifts and opportunities I couldn't have imagined for myself, and in hindsight, You shielded me from desires that might have led me astray.

Thank You for giving me a heart of worship and for calling out the prophetic.

"My frame was not hidden from You, When I was being formed in secret, And intricately and skillfully formed [as if embroidered with many colors] in the depths of the earth. Your eyes have seen my unformed substance."

I am humbled to be a vessel for Your messages and love. Thank You for showing me there is power when I surrender. It's in those moments of release that I've witnessed Your miracles and felt Your grace most profoundly. Thank You for giving me grace, more than I deserve. Your grace is an unmerited gift, a constant reminder of Your boundless love and forgiveness. I am endlessly thankful for Your compassion, which lifts me up in times of despair and shines a light on my darkest moments.

PREFACE:

Prayer of Gratitude

(PSALM 139:13-18, AMP)

"For You formed my innermost parts; You knit me [together] in my mother's womb."

I thank You, God, for putting a song in my heart and grace upon my lips. Thank You for protecting me, even from myself. There have been times when I've made choices that I later regretted, but Your guiding hand has kept me on the path of righteousness. It's a reminder that I'm not alone in this journey, and can always rely on Your steadfast presence to shield me from my own weaknesses and shortcomings.

"I will give thanks and praise to You, for I am fearfully and wonderfully made."

Thank You for teaching me You will fight my battles, and I need only to be still. Sometimes, life's challenges seem insurmountable, but You've shown that surrendering to Your will and trusting Your plan is the ultimate source of strength. In those moments of instilled a resilience that continues to strengthen me. Sometimes, the most challenging paths lead us to the most profound healing and personal growth, allowing our stories to be filled with the victory of overcoming.

NEW SCARS

Old scars, the ones that have faded with time, no longer hold the same weight of relevance. They are a part of me, ingrained in my personal history, but they take a back seat to the new scars and evoke less of a reaction than they did in the past. Those older scars are like chapters in a book I've already read.

But new scars challenge me, cause me to question my identity, and force me to adapt to an ever-changing narrative of my existence. Whether created from the result of a physical injury, a painful surgery, or even a deep emotional wound, fresh marks serve as a reminder that life is constantly in flux. They force us to confront our vulnerability and adapt to the unexpected.

It's interesting to think that some people willingly pay for scars or tattoos to adorn their bodies, and society often romanticizes these choices. Yet, when our scars come from battles we never chose, they can be met with judgment and criticism. All scars should be embraced, celebrated even, because they symbolize and represent our battles, our strength, and the uniqueness of our life experiences. Today, I'm happy to say, I've come to accept my scars, both old and new, as an integral part of who I am. They may not always look aesthetically pleasing, but they're a testament to my story, and I wouldn't trade them for anything.

While I don't actively seek new scars, when they appear, I'm learning to deal with them and give myself grace. It's an ongoing journey, one I'm discovering is more about the process of healing from those scars than trying to prevent them. I've often found myself striving to build a life that's designed to be impervious to hardships or any potential scarring. I've tried to protect various aspects of my life from receiving any more scars or wounds, whether they are physical or emotional.

It's a natural instinct, really, wanting to shield oneself from pain and suffering. Who wouldn't prefer a life free from heartbreak and disappointment? Yet, that cannot be, as the realness of life comes crashing in: no matter how hard we try we cannot control every circumstance, and we certainly can't control the actions and choices of those around us. We only have the ability to control our responses to those circumstances. We only can control how we choose to embrace our scars and the stories that created them.

No matter how hard we try, we will experience moments when we get hurt, when life leaves its mark on us, often in unexpected and uncontrollable ways. This can be frustrating and disheartening, leaving us feeling vulnerable and exposed. However, what I've come to understand is that life is not about avoiding these scars but learning how to respond to them. What matters is the process of learning to heal and, equally important, learning to give grace to others who are also in the process of healing. We're all imperfect, and we all carry our own scars and wounds, some visible, others hidden beneath the surface.

It's in these shared moments of vulnerability and empathy that we find connection and understanding. We can support one another as we navigate the complexities of life—scars and all. I don't seek new scars, but I no longer fear them. I've come to see scars as an integral part of my growth and transformation, reminding me that life is about the journey, the healing, and the grace we extend to ourselves and others along the way.

BEAUTIFUL SCARS

I am beautifully scarred because my imperfections tell a story of resilience, healing, and God's unyielding power and mercy. God, the master artist, took those broken pieces, inside and out, and mended what was meant to be a permanent void, turning it into a work of art.

God didn't just fix what was broken, but He transformed it into something that radiates His glory. My scars are no longer a mark of destruction but a symbol of His divine intervention. My story is miraculous, a story of God's handprint upon my life—a life that was once meant for death and destruction, but now it is teeming with life and purpose. I've become a living testament to His grace and a reflection of His love.

Through my scars and my story, I want to offer life and hope to those who may be struggling with their own battles. The most challenging trials can be overcome, brokenness can be mended, and even in our darkest moments, we can find a glimmer of light because there is hope. I share my story, not as a victim, but as a victor. I desire to cheer you on in this race of life, to remind you that no matter how broken or scarred you may feel, there is beauty in your story waiting to be unveiled. Just as God turned my scars into a masterpiece, He can do the same for you. Embrace your scars, for they are the chapters of your life that reveal the strength and beauty within you.

Sometimes I look in the mirror and don't see any scars, just a reflection of gratitude. Other times, I look in the mirror and see nothing but the scars etched into my skin and soul. The imperfections, the battle wounds, they all come into sharp focus. But there's a small voice inside me, a voice of reason and self-love, that whispers softly, assuring me that my scars are beautiful to those who love me.

This message of self-love isn't one I've come up with on my own. It's echoed through the unconditional love of God, Scripture, my family, and my doctors. They've shown me that my worth isn't determined by my physical appearance. It's rooted in the depth of my character, the kindness in my heart, and the resilience that these scars represent.

My beautiful scars are a work of art, a living masterpiece painted by the experiences and challenges I've faced. Let my scars speak to you, and maybe, just maybe, they can help you feel brave enough to show your beautiful scars too.

"And in Your book were all written the days that were appointed for me, When as yet there was not one of them [even taking shape]."

Thank You for closing doors and bringing me into a better place. When one door closes, You open another. I've seen the truth in this time and time again. Your guidance has led to unexpected, wonderful opportunities and moments of growth.

Thank You for holding me now and holding my future. In the embrace of Your love, I find solace and security. Knowing You are with me today, tomorrow, and forever fills me with hope and confidence.

"How precious also are Your thoughts to me, O God! How vast is the sum of them! If I could count them, they would outnumber the sand."

Thank You that greater days are before me than behind me: the best is yet to come. I thank You and praise You because I am fearfully and wonderfully made, even when I don't believe it. Despite my doubts and insecurities, You see the beauty in me. Your unwavering love reminds me that I am a masterpiece of Your creation, and for that, I am eternally grateful for my beautiful scars.

"When I awake, I am still with You."

PART I

CHAPTER ONE

The Promise

Butterflies flutter in my stomach, nerves setting in before I step onto the stage. My dad's encouraging words replay in my mind, reminding me that this feeling is a good thing and will help me focus on sharing my story. As I wait for my turn to speak, alone with my thoughts and my anticipation building, I can't help but reflect on my life that brought me here from a small village in Guatemala. It hasn't always been easy or beautiful, but I'm grateful for every step that led me to this moment. I start to envision my life unfolding like a movie, and I can hear myself narrating these exact words in my mind:

> I have been told that babies who are born in developing countries with a deformity can be considered a shame upon their families, and some are left to die. For some reason, these developing countries seem to have more than their share of infants with deformities. That could have been where my story ended—but God had other plans.

As I hear myself narrating, I see Nate, my husband; our three young boys, Ethan, Caleb, Eli; and myself driving through a beautifully winding road, eclipsed by the picturesque scene of trees gracefully bowed under the weight of snow and icicles sparkling in the winter sunset.

A blanket of white covers everything, resembling a postcardlike winter landscape. Anticipation permeates the air, and the atmosphere is brimming with love and excitement for the cherished moments that await us at my parents' house for Christmas. A gathering of twenty family members would soon greet us. As we drive, our hearts fill with the excitement of being together, playing competitive games, and experiencing the fun and chaos that accompanies any gathering of the Thompson family. It may be loud and a bit crazy—there's a constant undercurrent of laughter—but it's undeniably the best of times. We're all eager to reunite with aunts, uncles, and beloved cousins.

Pulling into my parents' home and making our way around the long, curved gravel driveway, my dad eagerly swings open the door as Nate puts the car in park. Dad is the first person to greet us, extending a much-needed helping hand with the boys. We step inside and hang up our scarves and coats, just in time to be immediately enveloped by a wave of greetings and warm hugs from family at the front door. Poinsettias decorate the staircase and the unmistakable scents of Christmas fill the house with the delightful fragrance of mistletoe and the comforting aroma of gingerbread cookies lingers in the air.

I suddenly snap back to reality and realize that it's taken me longer than I would like to admit to understand that life is about the journey, not just the destination. Truthfully, I will be learning this for the rest of my life.

I look out at the audience, and I tell my story.

And now I tell it in this book. I invite you behind the curtain of my life to witness the moments that have shaped me—the trauma, abandonment, rejection, identity, shame—how each contributed to the scars worn today, and to acknowledge those who played a pivotal role in saving my life.

LAS MONTAÑAS (THE MOUNTAINS)

On November 14, 1981, I was born in a quaint village nestled in the heart of the Sierra Madre Mountains, a three-day journey from Guatemala City. This village located high in the mountains, surrounded by valleys and crystal-clear rivers, is embraced by dense cloud forests. The region's fertile soil has long been dedicated to cultivating coffee, corn, and banana orchards. Over time, some agricultural lands have transitioned into lush green rainforests, while others remain vital for food production and supporting the livelihoods of villagers. This village lacked modern amenities; no electricity or plumbing, and no grocery stores. The only water source was a stream that lay a considerable distance from the houses, requiring people to walk a long way to reach the clear water while balancing a large water jug on their head. Despite these challenges, the community thrived through physical labor and had a deep connection to the natural beauty that surrounded them.

I was the sixth child born to Rita and Jesús Molina, and the pregnancy had been relatively uneventful without complications. Rita had already given birth to multiple children, all easy and unscarred, so they were joyfully anticipating my arrival. After taking my first breath to let out a cry, the midwife was the first to notice the birth defect. Speechless, she just stared at me, until Jesús looked over her shoulder and noticed as well. Seconds stretched by as Jesús and the midwife couldn't find the words to speak through their shock. Not sure how to explain to his wife what was wrong, he stalled for as long as possible. Rita asked to see me, so he gently placed me in my mother's arms. She held me close and was immediately overcome by what she saw, and tears began to flow. Her eyes focused on my bilateral cleft lip and palate. This meant I had no upper lip and no bone structure in the roof of my mouth, and it was far worse than just a cosmetic concern. Tears continued to stream down Rita's face. But Jesús, in the most endearing voice, looked into her eyes and said, "She is going to live, and I am going to do everything I can to save her!"

In a country with limited resources and widespread poverty, this condition posed a significant challenge. The absence of an upper lip made it impossible to nurse, and in a place with no access to formula or specialized care, it meant they had no way to feed me. The chance of survival for a child like me was near zero, and even if I did survive, it would mean a life of constant struggle and humiliation. My parents were heartbroken and terrified of this grim reality. They now were faced with a situation that seemed like another mountain in front of them. With no other options available, they resorted to an act of desperation by soaking a rag in breast milk and squeezing droplets into my mouth. I can only imagine the despair in their eyes as they watched their fragile, deformed child crying endlessly from hunger. However, it didn't take long for the effects of malnutrition to take their toll. I grew weaker, and soon, my loud cries turned to a faint whimper. It was a silence that spoke volumes, signaling the severity of the situation. It must have been excruciating to see their child dying before their eyes. But in desperation, Jesús and Rita continued to fight for me. Jesús wrapped me in a blanket, gathered what little supplies he had, held me close, and made the choice not to just see the mountain in front of him, but walk down it. The journey took him down the mountain trail three miles to a creek, which is where the dirt road began. It was several miles on the dirt road out to the byway. Then 140 kilometers (about one hundred miles) into Guatemala City, to find help.

Each step was filled with determination and purpose. It's difficult to fathom the emotional and physical strain he must have endured, knowing I was hungry and entirely dependent upon him. The weight of that responsibility, combined with the uncertainty of not being able to provide sustenance, must have been heartbreaking. Even with Jesús's experience as a father, the circumstances he now found himself in were completely foreign and undoubtedly overwhelming. The love he bore for me was a driving force, pushing him through the most challenging of terrains and circumstances.

Exhausted, Jesús stumbled into the bustling heart of Guatemala City with me fast asleep in his arms, worn out from the long journey and relentless hunger. While Jesús had been to Guatemala

City before, this time he was desperate, so he tried to calm his mind and reorient himself to the city. The city's enormity was overwhelming, and the busy streets were filled with people and commotion, seemingly stretching on forever through the endless sounds and chaos.

Finally, Jesús arrived at a hospital with my body held tightly in his arms. His eyes filled with an urgent and frenzied determination as he scanned the surroundings for anyone who could assist. He knew I was on the brink of death and every minute mattered. With every ounce of strength remaining, he held me up to the first doctor he spotted. The doctor's response and the actions that followed would determine whether I would be rescued from the brink of death or if my struggle for survival would continue.

The doctor, with a grave expression on his face, took one look and shook his head, his words piercing through the heavy air, "There's no one in this hospital who can perform the surgery your child needs."

My father's shoulders slumped with the weight of helplessness. The room seemed to grow darker; the prospect of losing me was too much to bear. But . . ."—he hesitated, as if reluctant to deliver the next blow—"the cost for the surgery would be a minimum of one thousand dollars."

A heavy silence hung in the air as the enormity of that amount registered in Jesús's mind. For a man whose annual income only provided enough money for survival, this was an insurmountable sum. He had worked tirelessly to provide for his family, but this was a financial chasm too wide to bridge. Jesús shrugged his shoulders, his face etched with defeat. As he turned away, tears welled up in his eyes, their silent trails running down his dirt-stained cheeks. He had to confront the hard truth—I was going to die. With a heavy heart and no other choice, he left the hospital with no hope for my survival. It was a gut-wrenching decision, one no parent should ever have to make.

Overcome with grief, he slumped to the hard ground outside the hospital doors. As he began weeping over my frail body, two men approached, seemingly out of nowhere.

"What's wrong, sir? Why are you crying?"

Between sobs, he motioned to my tiny body in his arms.

One of the men asked, "May we take a look?"

Hesitantly, Jesús pulled the blanket from my face, and the two men exchanged a knowing glance. Then one man said, "We know of a place that can help. There is an orphanage called Casa Guatemala. They help children like yours."

Jesús's eyes brightened with this sound of hope. "Is this true?"

"Yes."

"There is hope for your little girl. She will survive. They can help your baby and return her home when she is well again."
Wiping the tears away from his face with the back of his hand, Jesús asked, "Please, show me where I can find this place! I don't have money to pay you, but I know God will repay you."

The two men led him to Casa Guatemala and said their good-byes as he entered the orphanage. He later tried to find the men so that he could thank them, but they were nowhere to be found, and no one claimed to have even seen them. I truly believe these two men, even angels perhaps, were sent by God to save my life.

He was greeted by a kind woman named Angie who was in charge of this place known for its care and support of children in need. She understood the desperate situation he was in. But he was now faced with the hardest decision of his life—one that would tear his heart apart. He was told that the only way I would survive was to surrender my care to Angie and the devoted staff at Casa Guatemala, as they would try to arrange the much-needed free medical care. He knew this decision might be the only hope I had, but it required him to entrust strangers, a hard task, no matter how kind and well-intentioned they might be. As hard as the decision was to leave me behind, he was reminded of the words he had spoken to Rita: "She will live and not die." There was hope.

CHAPTER TWO

El Milagro

(THE MIRACLE)

When I arrived at Casa Guatemala, I was just three days old with little substance in my dying body, fighting to survive. Angie and her small team did everything within their means and knowledge to provide a chance for me to live, but it became a struggle I will never fully understand.

My massive bilateral cleft lip and palate involved two severely complex fistulas or openings on my upper lip and the roof of my mouth. The openings extended from the back of my mouth through the bone all the way to my nose. This condition occurs during early fetal development when the tissue that forms the lip and palate fails to fuse properly.

Since my birth defect made something as basic as feeding a difficult task, as I could not latch onto a bottle or a breast, I had to rely on a makeshift method that was as delicate as it was essential. Angie and her team fed me by carefully dripping milk into my mouth, hoping it would trickle down the back of my throat, allowing sustenance I so desperately needed.

But it wasn't a simple or straightforward process. Every time I cried out in hunger or pain, the defective palate made it nearly impossible to swallow properly. The milk they painstakingly provided me often pooled in the back of my throat, causing me to choke and sputter. It was a terrifying sensation; I was essentially drowning in the nourishment that was meant to save me. The more I cried, the harder it became to feed me, creating a heartbreaking cycle of frustration, hunger, and discomfort. Imagine the worry and exhaustion that Angie and her team must have felt as they tirelessly tended to me. They were, literally, sustaining my life one drop of milk at a time.

Now a battle against the clock, my condition required urgent medical care. Constant crying and the never-ending cycle of hunger and discomfort left me utterly exhausted until I would collapse into a fitful sleep. It was the only respite I had from the relentless challenges caused by my birth defect.

Jesús and Rita made it a point to visit me at Case Guatemala as frequently as possible. Despite the financial strain of leaving their orchard, which meant a loss in income, their love compelled them to visit. It was during these occasional visits that I received the physical touch and nurture my infant body craved. While Angie and her team were doing the best they could to keep me alive, there simply wasn't enough time for them to also give the human affection so vital for the survival of an infant. They had many other children dependent on their care.

At the close of each visit, Jesús and Rita would place me back into my cold, lonely crib, which was currently my home, and they would look at each other anxiously, both struggling with doubt and wondering whether I would live or die. At two months old, I barely weighed as much as a newborn, tipping the scale at just eight pounds. The odds seemed impossible, but they believed I was going to live. Unbeknownst to them, nearly four thousand miles away in Ritzville, Washington, the hearts of another family were being moved.

THE DECISION

Born in the post-war era of the 1940s and raised in the foothills of Mount Baker, nestled in the picturesque town of Bellingham, Washington, James Rea Thompson, known as Rea (pronounced Ray), was the middle child among his nine siblings. From a young age, he was instilled with the values of hard work, being good-hearted, and the importance of keeping one's word. Like many elementary kids, he spent his summers picking strawberries for three weeks, earning anywhere from one hundred to three hundred dollars. But his first "real" job came in the eighth grade, when he worked for a landscaping company that sold plants, operated greenhouses, and did yard work on Saturdays.

Throughout his upbringing, regular church attendance wasn't a common practice for Rea since he didn't see its relevance. However, his ambivalent attitude against church was not appreciated by Judi Swann, his high school sweetheart. Judi's grandmother had been taking her to church since Judi was ten, instilling in her the importance of a deep faith. Despite this difference, Rea and Judi married at the young ages of eighteen and nineteen.

A significant turning point occurred for Rea early one morning when Dick Frey, a friend staying with them, caught Rea's attention. Dick was not only an ex-pro football player and avid athlete, but also someone Rea admired in every way.

Early one morning, before everyone else was awake, Rea observed Dick reading his Bible at the breakfast table, sparking his interest. This experience prompted a shift in Rea's perspective, especially concerning the idea of having a need for God. Despite Rea's previous reservations, he felt strongly that Shelly, their infant daughter, should be exposed to the teachings of a church community.

It wasn't long before Rea was confronted about his own relationship with God, and he made the personal choice to follow Jesus. Several years later, now with four children — Shelly, Shannon, Tyler, and Piper — Rea and Judi moved to Texas on a leap of faith so he could attend seminary at Southern Methodist University. After completing his studies, they returned four years later to Ritzville, Washington, where Rea took on a pastoral role in the United Methodist Church.

One of Rea's greatest passions was to serve people, and this was evident in his sincere desire to provide love and support to those in need during hospital stays. On a typical brisk Pacific Northwest afternoon, while Rea was making his visitation rounds at the Spokane Hospital, an unexpected encounter forever changed the course of the Thompson family's lives — and mine. Turning the corner of the hospital corridor, Rea ran into one of his high school classmates, Cris Embleton. In her excitement, she began emphatically telling Rea that she'd started a new organization, Heal the Children. Intrigued, Rea couldn't help but inquire further.

Cris explained with radiant enthusiasm, "We are a ministry that connects children in desperate need of lifesaving surgeries with the medical care and assistance they require. One of the responsibilities is to find families willing to foster these children while they undergo critical surgeries here in the States, all accomplished by donating services and housing." Rea observed the dedication and compassion fueling Cris's work. In a seemingly spontaneous moment, Cris's gaze sharpened as she turned to him and posed a life-changing question. "So, are you ready to take in a foster child?"

After deep consideration, he responded. "Let Judi and I pray about this, and we'll get back to you."

As Rea walked into their modest parsonage, he found Judi in a back room laying tile flooring. No job was ever too big or too small for the Thompson family. They took deep pride in every home they lived in, and this scene was all too familiar.

"Speed (Rea's affectionate nickname for Judi), you'll never guess who I ran into today at the hospital. Cris!"

Judi frowned. "Who?"

"You know, Cris Embleton from high school," Rea added. "Guess what she's doing? She started an organization that helps children from around the world in need of medical help, and she asked if we want to foster a child."

Judi put the tile trowel down, stood up, and thought for a minute. "Well, that's definitely something we would need to pray about."

A few days went by, and after the entire Thompson family prayed about this big decision, they all felt a peace about saying yes, so they called Cris to inform her they would love to foster a child when one was available. Cris was ecstatic and told them she would send over a list of names for them to look over. They should pick a child's name that seemed to jump off the page.

That night, they sat down with their four children and showed them the list of names. Each child perused the list like a Christmas toy catalog. Tyler was the first to see a young boy named Juan Carlos, who was from Guatemala and in need of leg surgery because of polio and scoliosis, which prevented him from walking. Tyler's eyes widened with the thought of having a temporary brother. One by one, the names on the list continued, until for some reason my name seemed to be highlighted. Shelly and Shannon said, "Mom, there's another baby on this list from Guatemala. Her name is Santos Camentina and she's not even two months old. She has something called a cleft palate. What's that?"

Piper asked, "Mom, how many can we get?"

Judi smiled. "Now, this isn't like getting a pet. These are kids who will need our help. Let's start with two and see where it goes from there."

After brainstorming and shouting out different names, they quickly agreed that both I and Juan Carlos were the two children they would foster. From that point, they decided to drop the "tina" from my name and call me Camen for short. With the paperwork completed and the procedures in motion, Rea, Judi, and the kids prepared their hearts for our arrival and awaited the call from Heal the Children.

It didn't take long for Rea to receive a call from Cris, informing him that I would be arriving at the Spokane International Airport that day! Rea, caught off guard, inquired about Juan Carlos, but Cris explained he had missed the flight. Unable to leave work at the last minute, Rea called Judi to ask if she could pick up the baby and emphasized the need to buy supplies since I would likely come with only what I was wearing.

Excitedly, Judi agreed to handle the preparations. Piper, sensing her mother's excitement, questioned if it was about the baby's arrival. Judi, brimming with joy, confirmed and instructed Piper to hurry and get Tyler, as they needed to leave now.

"I can't wait to hold her, Mom! I am so excited!" Piper bounced up and down. "Tyler! It's time to get in the car. We're going to meet Camen!"

The hour-long ride to the airport was laced with laughter, silly songs, and endless questions from Tyler and Piper, whose curiosity regarding the new temporary addition to their family was insatiable. The sounds of the airport and overhead announcements were completely ignored as Judi, holding Piper's and Tyler's hands, raced toward the arrival gate.

Glancing through the glass window, they watched the Western Airlines plane, now known as Delta, pull into the gate. A wave of joy, excitement, and curiosity surged inside them as they witnessed the doors opening and individuals emerging one by one. Minutes passed slowly. Judi looked for anyone in a uniform holding a baby. Then, she saw a flight attendant escort, the wife of a pilot, who had volunteered to accompany the baby exiting the tunnel, and she knew it was me.

"Mrs. Thompson?" the woman asked.

Judi raced toward her with Piper and Tyler close behind. "Yes, I'm Judi Thompson. Is this Santos?" Judi held out her arms. The woman nodded as she gently handed Judi my tired little body, wrapped in a pink crocheted outfit.

"Thank you so much for caring for her during the flight." Judi moved the blanket from my face. I was told my eyes flashed open at the sound of her voice, and Judi was immediately lost in the depth of my large, brown eyes staring into hers.

The kids were eager to meet and see me as well. Judi knelt down to let them get a closer look. When Tyler saw me, he was stunned yet curious and didn't know what to say. But Piper, age nine, took one look at me and saw what looked like a ball of tissue and bone at the end of my nose and the gaping hole in my mouth. She looked back at her mom, and with tears flooding her little eyes, she bolted away in a rush.

Handing me to the pilot's wife, Judi followed Piper into the restroom.

"Piper . . . Piper, Mom is here. Mom is here."

After some dry heaving, Piper came out of the locked stall, sniffling with tears streaming down her face. "My tummy hurts . . . I didn't know, Mom. I didn't know . . . my tummy hurts. I don't feel so well."

Judi bent down to her level, wiped away her tears, and gently embraced Piper with a tight hug. "Mom is here."

"Mom, how are we going to help her? How are we going to do this?" Piper asked.

Judi looked her in the eyes. "Piper, I don't know how, but I know we just are, and it's going to be okay." Their eyes met and searched each other deeply. Piper realized that her mom didn't have all the answers either, but she trusted her and knew it was going to be okay—just like she said. Taking a deep breath and gathering her courage, Piper walked out with her mom's hand in hers and returned to Tyler and the woman holding me.

The pilot's wife and the stewardess said their goodbyes and wished Judi all the best as they handed over my small bag with hardly anything in it. Judi and her children made their way back to the car. In the back seat sat Piper, a baby on a pillow (since they didn't have car seats at that time), and Tyler. Piper would occasionally steal glances from the corner of her eye, looking at the gap on my face before turning to the window while trying to process everything.

Tyler managed to make me smile, and Piper, out of the corner of her eye, caught a glimpse, not of the gap in my mouth, but of my brown eyes meeting her own big, brown eyes. She then realized two other dimples were on the sides of my face.

"Mom, she has the biggest dimples! Can I hold her?"

Mom, looking in the rearview mirror, nodded. "Yes, just hold her gently."

"Okay."

Piper carefully picked me up and held me in her lap, staring into my eyes. That moment forever connected us. Not wanting to miss a turn, Tyler asked if he could hold me next. Our eyes met, and a soft smile spread across his face. In a playful tone, he called me "Camarones," which I would later find out meant shrimp in Spanish.

When they arrived home, they realized just how small I was when Rea held me in the palm of his hands. None of the baby clothes or diapers fit, but Piper brought out her favorite baby doll and offered its clothes for me.

Soon after my arrival, the Thompsons noticed that Camentina was legally written Clementina on my paperwork. They became concerned that my name would be too closely associated with the song, "Clementine," so they opted to name me Camen. However, they decided Camen still sounded too big, so they simply called me Camey Joy.

CHAPTER THREE

El Regalo

(THE GIFT)

Since the moment of my arrival into the Thompson home, they embraced me as their own. I was home. However, it was made very clear by Heal the Children that the possibility of adoption was out of the question. Their chief mission was to bring in children for a brief time to receive medical care and then have them promptly returned home. As the initial days turned into months, the realities of the medical condition became more evident, and it was clear that surgeries would be extensive and ongoing—not for months, but years, because the bones would shift and change as growth occurred.

The first surgery was just the beginning with a series of intricate procedures that would stretch across years. Knowing this, the Thompsons resolved to face this journey head-on. Their love was the catalyst to fight for the medical care and nurture I desperately needed.

Returning to Guatemala between surgeries for my care was technically an option, but the practicalities seemed daunting. The ongoing need for surgeries and medical attention meant that going back posed significant risks. Infections lurked as potential threats, and paperwork hurdles could result in complications. Then there was the unsettling possibility that returning to America may be hindered—which would put an end to the lifesaving surgeries that I needed. Added to the challenges was the backdrop of a civil war ravaging Guatemala during that time. The wisdom of not taking me back to a country in turmoil, coupled with the pressing medical needs, provided a clear decision for the Thompsons. Armed with love and guided by the counsel of medical professionals, the Thompsons realized that my well-being dictated staying with them. With hearts wide open, they embraced the responsibility, making a commitment based on unconditional love.

And it was a responsibility with my unique needs. Originally, the doctors wanted me to weigh a minimum of twelve pounds before undergoing the first surgery. However, at ten months old I weighed just ten pounds, and getting to twelve pounds seemed like an insurmountable feat. The weight of those trying times was shared collectively by each member of the Thompson family. They would take turns holding me close while wrapped in a blanket adorned with pictures of young girls from around the world. Their presence provided security and comfort as they dedicated countless hours to feeding and caring for me.

The feeding process was definitely the most difficult task. Initially, the Thompsons weren't even sure how to get me to swallow milk properly. In a moment of sheer providence, Judi stumbled on a medical book that discussed this exact dilemma. The journal described successful feedings of infants with a cleft palate by using a special type of nipple that allowed milk to easily bypass the cleft and drip down the back of an infant's throat.

After searching without success for the specific device, Judi headed to the nearest pharmacy where she stumbled upon a "duck-billed" nipple that seemed similar to the one in the book. With this attachment, feeding was no longer an impossible feat—but it still required round-the-clock dedication and painfully slow progress. It took two hours to feed me four ounces.

This concerted effort was crucial to nurturing me back to health, but I can only imagine the emotional toll it took on my new family, as they witnessed my struggles with pain and hunger. During this time they discovered the power of a song! My family sang, "Jesus, Name Above All Names," and from the very first word, "Jesus," my cries would miraculously fade, and my body would relax with an immediate sense of peace.

While I struggled to gain the much-needed weight for the first surgery, the doctors wanted me to wear a custom-made plastic helmet with a buckle strap that went under my nose. This would apply pressure to shift the nodule of bone back into alignment. Wanting to give more comfort, Judi sewed a cushion along the strap to prevent it from hurting my mouth and surrounding tissue. I'm told I was not a fan of this device; yet as a baby, little did I know the benefits it would bring down the road. When photos were taken, Judi would place a pretty bonnet on my head to cover the helmet, but you could still see the strap across my lip that forced the bone downward.

Even though I was not gaining the required weight the physicians desired for the first surgery, they finally agreed to proceed. So, at a whopping ten pounds, my first surgical intervention focused on addressing the cleft lip. With precision, the surgeon pushed the ball of bone on my lip down, which was extremely difficult and delicately incised on each side of the cleft, extending from the lip to the nostril. The two sides of my lip were meticulously sutured together. To do this, the surgeon used tissue from the surrounding area to close and reshape the lip. They also repositioned the muscle in my lip. This intricate maneuver was essential for reconstructing the circular muscle around the tiny mouth at a later surgery. Typically, during this surgical step, additional support for the nose is also provided. However, because of the unique configuration of my jaw and nose bones, the surgeon decided to wait on this particular aspect of the procedure until a later date. After this grueling surgery, the doctor waited three months before performing the next surgery to lift my nose. The surgeries performed were cutting-edge then, which was exciting and nerve-wracking for Rea and Judi.

    The result, however, had an unintended effect. Since Rea and Judi had always embraced the distinctiveness of my cleft lip and palate, as that was how I was known and loved, they weren't prepared for the emotional impact surgical transformation would have on them. As I emerged from the operating room after surgery, and the nurse handed me over to Judi with my newly closed lip, an unexpected reaction overcame her, catching her off guard. The sight of my lip closed was so unfamiliar, she struggled to articulate the sensation, likening it to the way animals sometimes reject their young when a noticeable change occurs.

    In retrospect, she acknowledged her comparison might sound odd, but it was the only way she could express the way she felt in that moment. The cleft had been a cherished feature and was now altered.

The absence of the familiar gap and signature big smile made me appear so different. She had grown to love that big, gapped smile!

As I lay in Judi's arms, staring at her, I uttered the word mum, and she began weeping tears of joy. This was the first time she had heard me say this word, and she realized the surgery had made speech possible for me. I am told there was not a dry eye in the room.

In that moment, she understood this was what I needed. The surgery was a success, and when I returned home, the Thompson family continued to treat me the same and shower me with love, whether there was a gap in my lip or not.

THE RING

In February 1983, Rea and Judi found themselves embarking on an unexpected adventure with three other couples, who were all fostering children from Heal the Children. Their mission was to travel to Guatemala to bring back eleven more children who would go into various host homes throughout the United States.

With limited financial resources, the couples hesitantly approached a travel agency to purchase tickets for the trip. Each ticket would cost about four hundred dollars, an overwhelming sum at the time. However, as they discussed the logistics with the travel agent, a call from Cris interrupted the conversation. Cris joyfully announced that she had secured free tickets for everyone, turning what seemed like an impossible endeavor into a reality.

Upon their arrival in Guatemala, the group faced unexpected challenges. Gathering the eleven children proved to be a chaotic process. When they reached the airport, they discovered that the tickets they had intended to purchase from the Guatemalan airline were no longer available because the airline had gone bankrupt. This unforeseen delay provided an opportunity for Rea and Judi to possibly meet Jesús and Rita.

The next day, while navigating through the bustling streets of Guatemala in a van with three other couples, Rea and Judi passed numerous small villages. Eventually, they turned down a particular road, then made a right turn, and encountered a woman and her son seeking a ride. Quick to extend kindness, Rea invited the woman and her son to join them.

Even though the van was full, the mother and son squeezed into the back with them. Rea mentioned, in what little Spanish he spoke, that they were searching for the parents of a child named Santos Clementina Molina Milian.

The woman's jaw dropped open. "I'm her aunt, Marta! I'm her dad's sister." Marta excitedly offered to guide them to their village.

Meeting Marta was miraculous, but when the van dropped Rea and Judi off on the corner of a dirt road to make their way up the mountain, they received another miracle. Rita and Jesús stood there holding bags filled with tamarindos that Jesús planned to sell down in the city! Judi spotted them and immediately recognized Rita as my biological mother. How she knew, she can't explain, but she simply said, "I just knew." Without hesitation, Rea, Judi, Rita, and Jesús ran toward each other. There was an immediate recognition, an understanding that went beyond words. Their arms wrapped around each other in a tight embrace, as if they were reuniting after a long separation, although until that moment, they were essentially strangers.

Amid their shared joy, someone asked how they would communicate, given the language barriers. Judi, with a knowing smile, responded, "We will communicate through love and tears."

They prepared to ascend the mountain on foot since there was only a trail going up the mountain, as cars were unable to navigate the dangerously steep and narrow road, but horses were provided. Judi had some experience with horses, but she was given a big, oversized umbrella to shield herself from the heat while managing the horse's reins.

Finding it comical, Judi jokingly suggested she should have walked instead. Jesús and Rita sent a messenger to run ahead and inform everyone of their arrival. During the journey up the mountain on a simple dirt trail, they stopped at a little shack selling every kind of soft drink imaginable.

After arriving at Rita and Jesús's home, Rita prepared chicken soup for lunch. Rea and Judi were deeply touched by the warmth and hospitality they received. Children approached the table, showing Rita and Jesús various chickens. Rita gave her approval, and after the meal, Rita tied two chickens by the feet and hung them over the horses—the chickens were a generous gift for Rea and Judi to take with them.

While they were visiting, Rea and Judi noticed a trickle of people gathering, and eventually, there were thirty or more in the group. However, one particular man standing off to the side caught Judi's attention. He was watching and observing everything. His eyes radiated a bright and beautiful shade of blue. Taking off his straw hat, he approached Judi, and with the kindest voice, told her he had been fervently praying to God, asking for their arrival one day. Through his broad smile, he said, "And God answered my prayers. Here you are!"

Judi let his words sink deep into her heart, comforted by the fact that others were praying for the entire situation as well.

During the meal, Judi wrestled with whether this would be the time she and Rea could ask if they could adopt me, but the right time never seemed to arrive. While Judi processed everything in her heart, her eyes kept looking down at the ring on her finger that she cherished so much. This ring was Judi's most treasured possession, given to her by her mother when her father passed away years before. It was a gold ring adorned with five swans affectionately reflecting Judi's maiden name, Swann.

Judi gazed tenderly at the ring, remembering the love of her mother and father. The ring held sentimental value beyond anything money could buy. As Judi pondered the idea of asking Rita to adopt me, her heart tightened with conflicting emotions. The weight of the decision pressed upon her, and her mind drifted to the ring adorning her finger. How would she feel if someone asked her to give up her ring, let alone her child? This thought caused Judi to question whether she could ever ask such a thing of Rita and Jesús. At that same moment, Judi felt like God was telling her to give Rita her ring as a gift of love, not as a transaction but as a testament of the depth of love and trust. Tears welled in her eyes as she determined to obey God, yet beneath her determination, she felt a wave of shame wash over her for even wrestling with the idea of parting with her ring. In an act of obedience, she twisted the golden swans off her finger and placed it gently into Rita's palm. Although Rita didn't understand the great sentimental value of the ring, something happened between their spirits, and an unbreakable connection was made. Rea and Judi didn't fully understand how God was moving, but they knew He was at work, and they trusted Him. The shared love between the two couples was enough. Rea and Judi left that day without asking if they could adopt me. Yet the beauty of Guatemala and its people had left them with a lasting impression.

THE CALL

A few weeks passed since the trip to Guatemala when Rea and Judi received a call. As they picked up the phone, they heard the familiar voices of Jesús and Rita on the other end. With great excitement, they navigated through a translator to understand the purpose of the call. Through the interpreter's words, Jesús conveyed a message that they had not expected. He spoke of the profound love he and Rita had witnessed when Rea and Judi visited their home. They knew in their hearts that I was greatly loved and cherished. He then made an unselfish and sacrificial offer that forever changed my life. He expressed that if Rea and Judi were willing to adopt, they would wholeheartedly give their blessing. Rea and Judi understood the seriousness of this offer and they marveled at the profound way God answered their prayer! They did not have to ask as I became a gift of unconditional love—a forever member of the Thompson family.

Rita and Jesús had one humble request. It wasn't a condition, but rather a plea. They asked that while embracing my new life, Rea and Judi would help keep the memories of my Guatemalan family alive in my heart as I grew. They didn't want me to forget the deep love they would always have for me no matter where I was or who raised me. They wished for a thread of continuity that would connect the two chapters of my life. With tears streaming down their faces and the awe of God filling their hearts, Rea and Judi said, "Why, of course!"

RECONCILING MY IDENTITY

Since as far back as I can remember, my parents were open about the fact that I was adopted, often explaining my story in a simple manner while sharing pictures of my biological family. "Camey, you have another mommy and daddy who love you very much," they would say.

One time, as Mom told me this beautiful story, I sat on her lap, held her cheeks with my hands, pushed the photo away, and insisted, "No, Mommy, you're my mommy." My parents were fulfilling a promise made to Rita and Jesús to keep their memory alive. However, in my heart and at such a young age, grasping the concept of adoption was difficult.

I initially dismissed the idea of adoption. After all, I didn't have a personal connection with Rita and Jesús, other than the pictures Mom and Dad had shown and the wonderful stories I'd heard about them. The language barrier posed a significant obstacle for communication, as my family spoke English while they spoke Spanish. Additionally, we were separated by countries.

The only parents that I'd ever known, loved, and trusted were Rea and Judi—my parents—and I couldn't imagine anything different.

Dad and my sister Piper took a trip to Guatemala, and that's a different story for another day. However, when he returned, he brought back a handpicked gift for me. I could sense his excitement in selecting the perfect present—an adorable Guatemalan doll with double braids, a white blouse, and a Guatemalan skirt, wearing a pair of brown sandals with a basket on her head. As he approached to give me the doll, I felt embarrassed because I wanted nothing to do with Guatemala and did not want to be identified as Guatemalan.

But with time, my understanding of adoption expanded, and I began to appreciate Guatemalan culture, although my appreciation remained a continent away. Letters from Rita and Jesús would arrive in the mail, and my parents would respond with updates. In an era before social media, this arrangement suited me fine because it allowed me to maintain a comfortable distance.

CHAPTER FOUR
The Beauty in the Pain

Beauty can be found in the midst of pain and suffering. However, when it's my own heart that bears the weight of suffering, seeing the beauty isn't always easy and it requires time. They say hindsight is 20/20, and I find truth in that wisdom. Having navigated through the challenges of twenty-three surgeries, some major while others smaller, and numerous medical interventions, I was left each time with an indelible scar, shaping not only my physical body but also the landscape of my mind.

During my early school years, it seemed like an unrelenting rhythm of one to two surgeries or procedures per year. In innocence, I used to find comfort and even excitement in visits to the doctor's office or the dentist. Back then, the love and care I received from medical professionals, coupled with the unwavering support of my family, made me feel uniquely special. I embraced life with a sense of confidence that could conquer anything. However, this idyllic perspective shattered when I encountered my first traumatic experience right before a surgery at the tender age of three years old. The once comforting and familiar environment of the medical world transformed into a realm of uncertainty and fear.

WHITE COATS

While what I faced was difficult, my feisty determination helped me deal with it. My mom has told me that I generally had an easygoing demeanor. However, a side of me emerged when I set my sights on something and encountered obstacles along the way. It was during these moments that my easygoing nature took a back seat, and a feistier and more determined side came out, causing me to become tenacious. Challenges and setbacks didn't deter; instead, they fueled my determination. In those instances, I was never one to back down easily.

Mom often emphasized that I was a survivor. She witnessed my ability to navigate through challenges, adapt to changing circumstances, and emerge stronger on the other side. It wasn't just about wanting something; it was about my God-given capacity to persevere. My feisty moments weren't just displays of determination; they were demonstrations of resilience, which would be needed for what I was about to face.

We eventually moved to Bremerton, Washington and, shortly after, went to a new doctor in nearby Tacoma who recommended a device to address some concerns about the closure of my palate. Little did we know how this seemingly harmless device would become a significant source of trauma. The medical transition wasn't as smooth as my parents had hoped, and my parents were not impressed with the new doctor. Despite their reservations, they continued with the recommended treatment plan, which involved the insertion of a device in the palate. This device had a more ambitious goal: to close the palate. So the surgery was scheduled.

I vividly recall the overwhelming fear that gripped me, at three years old, as I lay waiting for the surgery in a sterile environment, surrounded by stark coolness, my hand clenched to my blanket, which I affectionately called "nite-nite." My nite-nite gave me a sense of peace in times of fear and isolation, but in a sudden and unsettling moment, it was snatched away by an anesthesiologist, leaving me feeling vulnerable and exposed. The abruptness of it all unleashed a torrent of tears. My mother watched helplessly from a distance, and I cried more with my arms extended to hers, wanting her tender comfort but unable to receive it. My mother protested, but at that point, her hands were tied, and she couldn't do much to change the situation. She felt heartbroken for me as she witnessed me being traumatized right in front of her eyes, and she was powerless to rescue me from the ordeal.

As the anesthesiologist took charge, he and two technicians held me down against a cold stretcher in one swift and unexpected moment. The sudden restraint of my arms and the ominous rise of the bed rails amplified my vulnerability. Suddenly and without any explanation, the anesthesiologist grabbed a mask and placed it over my face. I felt pressure as he held my head down on the bed with force. Panic gripped my belly and rose to my chest as each breath became a struggle. I turned my face in a futile attempt to escape the overwhelming sensation of suffocation, but the grip of the anesthesiologist and the assisting technicians held firm in a desperate struggle for control. The air felt thin and the instinct to survive kicked in with a fierce determination. My cries that reverberated were a silent plea for understanding and mercy. I felt like I could not breathe, yet I was fighting—fighting to stay alive.

Looking back, he should have been fired for what he did. I'm not sure exactly what would have prompted his frustration with a child: Was it because I had a different skin color? Could it have been because I had a deformity? Was this just his own prejudice? Or was it because I was scared and crying, or having a difficult moment? Or was it possibly that he was having a bad day? Regardless of the reason, this moment in time forever scarred my memory.

After this traumatic experience, whenever I would see someone in a white coat, it immediately triggered anxiety and fear. As a result of the trauma I experienced from the mask, I now request to undergo my surgeries without the mask, consisting of nitrous oxide, and request to have the IV placed beforehand, even though it is more painful. In my opinion, there seemed to be no other viable option. I had experienced trauma before I even realized what trauma was. As I grew older, I became terrified of needles more than the post-surgery pain. Yet, outwardly, I appeared to be tough (most of the time) because I thought toughness was necessary for survival. Whenever I was in the arms of my parents, I felt safe to let my guard down and was able to freely express my feelings.

UNDER THE KNIFE

Whenever the date of new surgery was approaching, my parents always explained everything they knew would happen in the most loving way and with as much detail as they could provide, with assurance that there was no other option but to undergo the necessary procedure. Their explanations were comforting since they made me feel well-prepared, but I was never excited about an impending procedure; my disability merely demanded it.

Occasionally, upon waking from surgery, I would momentarily forget what had just happened. However, other times I would immediately recall the surgery and wake up to that harsh reality. Sometimes I could also remember the extubation, the removal of the endotracheal tube. This process could be uncomfortable and, at times, even painful, causing discomfort in the throat along with a momentary feeling of not being able to catch your breath or swallow. My mouth and throat always felt dry, like I desperately needed water.

Waking up from surgery was always a disorienting experience, filled with fragments of awareness. Often, the first thing was the intense brightness of the lights overhead, piercing through grogginess. The sterile, clinical white of the room seemed to amplify the harshness of those lights. The chill in the air was another stark reminder of the hospital setting. I could feel it against my skin, adding to my foggy head. Sometimes the nurses were kind enough to wrap my cold, little body with a warm blanket, which always felt comforting.

Slowly regaining consciousness, I would become aware of the physical restraints on my wrists since they were typically tied to the bed rails, a precautionary measure that emphasized the reality of the surgical process and the importance of not touching my mouth. The beeping sounds surrounding me were a constant reminder of what I'd just experienced. Amid the beeping and the sterility of the environment, voices would reach my ears, telling me the surgery was over. Remnants of the procedure lingered in the form of ointment that was meant to protect my eyes during surgery, which sometimes made it feel as if my eyes had been glued shut. I would force them open and gaze through the foggy goo that temporarily obscured my vision, trying to better take in my surroundings.

In those moments of uncertainty and vulnerability, my hands instinctively tried to reach out, desperately searching for the comfort of my nite-nite, which was more than just a piece of fabric. Sometimes the hospitals would have the blanket at my side by the time I woke up, while other times the blanket wouldn't arrive until my dad and mom gave it to me in the recovery room. The emphasis I placed on that simple blanket might seem disproportionate to an outsider, but for me, it was a profound source of security. The touch of the fabric against my skin provided a deep sense of comfort, grounding me in the midst of uncertainty. The familiar scent anchored me and made me feel safe and secure.

FIGHTING SHADOWS OF DOUBT

The severity of the surgeries was daunting enough, but to make matters even more challenging, a grim-faced doctor cast a shadow of doubt over the trajectory of my life. The doctor spoke to my parents as if he had no concern about me hearing his words. "Camey's case is severe," he announced abruptly so everyone in the room heard his voice. "The prospect of extensive speech therapy is inevitable, and she might not be able to talk due to the severely complex fistula still in her mouth." The doctor's prognosis was grim, to say the least, and hearing his words ended up leaving an emotional scar on my life, a trigger for my sensitivity to hearing others talk about me—which became a frequent occurrence.

The stark reality was that my ability to communicate effectively through speech remained unknown, leaving my parents to grapple with the uncertainty of whether I would be able to talk clearly at all. I spoke with a severe lisp that sounded more nasally and often only my family could decipher what was being said. The mention that I would most certainly need ear tubes added another layer to the intricate web of medical concerns. As the gravity of my condition unfolded through the words of medical professionals, my parents realized that this was only the beginning of the intense journey through an emotional and physical minefield that lay ahead.

CHAPTER FIVE

The Call

At the tender age of five, I don't recall ever praying what some call the "Sinner's Prayer" or a special prayer to be "saved" because I knew deep in my heart that Jesus was mine and I was His for as long as I can remember. I knew He was real and died and rose again on the third day. I also knew I didn't have to be baptized to belong to Him, but I had a strong desire to follow Jesus's example. I was terrified to submerge my face under water, a requirement for baptism by immersion. I'd asked my dad before being baptized if I could wear floaties around my arms, just in case. As he helped take my floaties off, he gently asked, "Do you trust me?"

Dad gently guided me toward the deeper end of the pool, and a sense of safety and security overwhelmed me. I felt comforted in hearing the gently swooshing water as we moved. I could feel its coolness against my skin and could sense the sacredness of this moment. With each step deeper into the water, my anticipation grew. Dad, my protector, comforter, strength, and provider asked, "Do you profess the Lord Jesus Christ as your Lord and Savior?"

Without hesitation, I responded with a resounding yes! My heart echoed the sincerity of the words. Then came the pivotal moment—the act that would mark my spiritual journey. I heard the words, "With much pleasure and joy, I now baptize you, Camey Joy, in the name of the Father, Son, and Holy Spirit." As the water surrounded me, a holy connection seemed to bridge Earth and Heaven. The act of baptism was so simple, yet the weight of that moment was profound.

Emerging from the water, I was met with a sudden and unexpected sensation. For a fleeting second, a brilliant light overwhelmed my senses, and the world around me disappeared. It was as if time stood still, and I found myself momentarily blinded by a heavenly light. In that brief instance, I couldn't see the people around me, but I felt a presence that transcended the physical realm—it was God's presence.

I experienced one of the most significant memories of my young life. It was a spiritual awakening, a moment of clarity that went beyond my age. Some might argue that I was too young to fully grasp the magnitude of what had transpired, but in my heart and soul, I did understand. Something wonderful had occurred, and I knew it would shape the course of my life forever. Looking back, my baptism was not just an act of obedience; it was a personal transformation. It instilled a sense of purpose and a connection to God in me, and it became a foundation upon which I would build my faith. This was a moment I would carry with me throughout my spiritual journey—one that was just starting.

HEARING THE VOICE OF GOD

By the time I was five, my family had moved to Roanoke, Texas, in the expansive Dallas-Fort Worth area. This brought on an internal battle. Here I lived in Roanoke, a small town in North Texas, with a beautiful upper-middle-class family whom I looked nothing like. I looked nothing like "my" family. Some adopted children can blend into their family easily; no one would ever know unless someone said they were adopted. But in my case, it was like I wore a sign with blinking lights, "I'm not from North Texas, and probably not from the USA. I'm a foreigner and most definitely wasn't born into this family." I so desperately wanted to fit in. Throughout my childhood, Mom fielded countless looks, questions, and stares from curious onlookers. Whenever someone would approach her and ask whether I was adopted, my mom would respond, "No, we are."

I knew I stood out as the only dark-skinned child in the school and possibly in the city of Roanoke. The rare instances when I saw people with darker skin than mine usually occurred when I ventured beyond the comfort of Roanoke into the rougher parts of town.

It can be typical for small towns not to be very diverse, but living among white people was comfortable because it was all I knew.

Despite that, my world was filled with new surroundings and adventures. However, amid the excitement of a new home, there was an ongoing chapter in my life that revolved around the legal intricacies of my adoption. My parents were in the process of finalizing the paperwork, which meant frequent trips to Dallas and Houston, where the attorneys responsible for the proceedings were located.

Not grasping the complexities of the legal matters that were taking place, I sensed an air of tension and anticipation. The attorneys in Houston played a pivotal role in connecting with Guatemalan attorneys for the adoption process, yet the interactions with them were far from straightforward. It felt as though they were leading my parents through a maze, offering promises and assurances without making tangible progress. It became apparent the legal process was not only emotionally taxing but also financially burdensome for my parents.

During those extra-long drives to Houston, the car became a sanctuary of shared moments between Mom and me. The hum of the car's engine and the rhythmic flow of the road provided a backdrop to conversations that, even at my young age, I understood were very important. My mother, a pillar of strength, navigated these legal challenges with determination. Her love was evident in every mile traveled and every question answered.

As we approached Houston for one of those crucial meetings, I felt a mixture of curiosity and apprehension. The city's towering skyscrapers and labyrinth of unfamiliar streets paralleled the legal maze my parents were navigating. The attorneys, elusive suit-wearing figures in my young mind, seemed to reside in a world where time moved slowly, progress was impeded, and paperwork held the key to my official place in the family.

As I peered into the countryside and its countless rolling hills and pastures, my mother, always in tune to my inner world, asked,

"Hey, Camey, what are you doing back there?" With a nonchalant casual demeanor, I shrugged. "Oh, nothing. I'm just talking with the Lord."

My mom smiled, her eyes meeting mine in the rearview mirror.

"Oh, what did He say?"

I didn't need a moment to ponder. The words flowed out, "He said one day I'm gonna sing all around the world, to tell others that Jesus is real and still performs miracles today."

You see, during this particular stage of life, I spoke with a lisp with a strong nasal tone, partially because of my severe underbite. My struggle to articulate my thoughts left most people perplexed by my attempts at communication. In the midst of this frustration, my family gave me unconditional love and support, and the fact that they could understand me was a great comfort. They became my linguistic interpreters, the ones who could decipher the intricate code of my words and expressions for others, and in a stroke of unconventional wisdom, my mom suggested that I use my emotions and thoughts through singing. I truly loved singing worship songs to Jesus, especially, "Jesus Loves Me."

So with her love and encouragement, I didn't doubt the truth of that statement: I was going to sing all around the world. My mom also never questioned or doubted this bold statement despite my young age. If anything, she embraced and encouraged those words even more. As we continued our drive, I couldn't resist the urge to express myself through song, and with each note and verse, Mom's support only intensified. It was as if she saw beyond the innocence of a five-year-old and recognized God's miraculous power at work in me and my voice.

Looking back on that time now, I realize it was a turning point—a moment etched into the story of my life. It was more than just a child singing; it was an encounter that would shape the course of my life. In that moment, God gave me the gift of singing, and from that point on, my voice changed as it became stronger and, even more importantly, anointed.

And in that same moment, the Lord planted the seeds of passion and purpose and called me into a lifelong ministry of worship. This early experience in life serves as a testament to the profound impact that a parent's support can have on a child's life. Mom's faith in my abilities and the belief that God had spoken, even at such a young age, laid the foundation for a lifetime of singing and worship that God had called me to. I was never the same!

HEALING CONFERENCE

It felt like a whirlwind, from the events of my baptism to hearing the voice of God and His call in my life, to when, at the tender age of six, I found myself commissioned. I recall the moment vividly when my parents took my siblings and me to a healing conference in New Orleans in 1988. As we settled into the stadium, surrounded by people anticipating the possibility of their healing, the sound of passionate speakers' words wove through the air like threads of hope. Their voices weren't harsh and loud but spoken with a normal cadence, and their words held authority.

It was great, but I was hungry. Because I was so tiny, whenever I became hungry, I literally felt as though I were starving and believed that I could possibly die. Mom would always thoughtfully pack a lunch box, and this was carried wherever we went. As I sat in the arena, feeling hunger pangs, I frantically dove into the contents of the lunch box, only to eat a few bites before I was satisfied. My snack was disrupted by what unfolded before me. The arena was filled with strangers, each carrying the hope of receiving healing—blind eyes, deaf ears, wheelchairs, and hospital stretchers arranged in rows. In front, below us, stood a blind man, his steps guided by a supportive hand. Up close, the whiteness of his eyes caught my attention because I'd never seen a blind person this close to me.

As the evening progressed, God's miraculous hand of healing danced throughout the stadium. Wheelchairs transformed into launching pads for newfound steps, and the blind man, once confined in darkness, now saw the world with unveiled eyes! Doubts melted away as the undeniable power of God became apparent in the room.

In that moment, a desire stirred within my heart. I longed to feel that touch, to experience the tangible presence that surrounded us. Yet, even as a young child, I wanted authenticity—I wanted Him.

Venturing from my mother's side, I approached a random woman praying for others and asked if she would pray for me. As her hand graced my head, I closed my eyes, reaching my hands toward Heaven. While I don't remember the exact words she spoke, I could see the same light that had touched me during my baptism; a profound peace surrounded my body as I was filled with the presence of His Spirit. Perhaps, at some point, I believed that God could take away the scars on my lip—I knew He could. Even though my physical scars weren't miraculously erased during that conference, God began the process of healing scars I didn't even know needed to be healed, though not the physical scars left by the cleft. That night remains etched in my memory as the night I realized that God is real and that miracles, just like those in the Bible, still exist today.

Upon returning home from the conference, my parents continued our nightly tradition of praying for me before bed. One particular night, I remember Mom's words filled with power as she prayed, "Camey, I pray for favor, discernment, and wisdom. I thank you, Lord, that she is going to travel to the nations you have called her to. Your voice is not just going to be a good voice that fills the room, but, Camey, your voice is anointed—a voice that sets you apart. Your voice will shift the atmosphere."

This marked the beginning of the race that the Lord had set before me. It wasn't immediate like I wanted, but I was called and set apart to share with others that God is real and still performs miracles today.

CHAPTER SIX

Not From Around Here

The way I remember, growing up in Roanoke was like living in a bubble. My childhood memories of living in Roanoke were filled with adventures. We seldom ventured outside of that small town, except to travel to Denton for speech therapy and then later to go downtown to visit the Dallas Children's Hospital, the dental hospital and many doctor visits.

Living with a Caucasian family, I rarely saw people with dark skin other than when I saw my own reflection, but even then, I didn't notice its golden dark hue. Thankfully, I didn't experience bullying because I was part of the Thompson family. Almost everyone knew, respected, and liked our family, which ensured my safety. Once in a while, I saw people passing through our community with darker skin that looked similar to mine. I began noticing people with my skin color who were featured on the covers of the National Geographic magazines lying on our dining room table.

Occasionally, I would receive disapproving looks from strangers or overhear murmurs about me. I wasn't always certain that they were talking about me, but it did feel as though I was the subject of discussion. It was challenging to discern whether it was because of my race, adopted status, cleft lip, or the way I spoke. Regardless, being excluded from those conversations was disheartening. And was another mark in a wound created from the doctor talking about me.

At some point, something changed about my reflection that now came into sharp focus in the mirror. I began to realize that I looked different from my family, and I started wearing a mental cloak of shame regarding my skin color.

Clearly, I had a strong desire to fit in and resemble my family. I felt this longing deep inside me. Whenever I encountered someone of a race like mine, it served as a reminder of my true identity, a reminder that I was not the same as my white family. Instead of embracing the beauty of being different, I held the scar of rejection and the need for acceptance.

THE MIRACLE CREAM

My family was truly a spectacle—incredibly outgoing, funny, competitive, athletic, and did I mention, beautiful? Since childhood, I've recognized the exceptional beauty of my siblings. I genuinely admired and appreciated their tall stature, beautiful hair, radiant skin—all the physical qualities I aspired to possess.

The Thompson girls were charming and popular wherever they went, attracting attention from all the boys. Tyler, the only boy in the wild bunch and a star football player for Northwest High School, also embodied all these qualities. He was funny and loyal, so girls were always vying for his attention as well.

On hot, sunny days, I would often catch my sisters heading out to the trampoline in their swimsuits, untying their backs and lounging, sometimes even falling asleep. But before stepping out, they would apply this white miracle cream that left their skin glowing, shiny, and stunning. Basking in the sun, listening to music, they would return with that beautiful, radiant skin I coveted. Watching in awe, I longed to look like them.

I have consistently approached challenges in my life with a "solution-oriented, never-let-anything-stand-in-my-way" attitude. However, this dilemma presented a unique challenge that I was determined to overcome: How can I look like my sisters? One day, when family members were preoccupied, I ventured into the kitchen and improvised stairs by pulling out the cabinet drawers so I could reach the top cabinet. There, I discovered the "miracle cream." I took scoops in my small hands and covered myself from head to toe. I quietly scampered outside to the trampoline looking like a summer snowman and lay down just like my sisters had done countless times before.

In the midst of patiently waiting for this miracle to take effect, I heard distant calls, "Camey . . . Camey," growing louder until I popped up. I rushed back inside with my miracle cream on. As I entered the room, my mom and sisters erupted into laughter, which didn't make me feel great. They asked, "Camey, what are you doing?" I barely squeaked out the humiliating words, "I'm trying to get white." I couldn't understand why they were laughing hysterically until they explained that they were actually trying to get their skin to look as tan and dark brown as mine. I was utterly perplexed as I gazed at them and then at myself. I couldn't comprehend why they desired to have a complexion as dark and brown as mine. It was beyond my childish understanding. Oh, and the "miracle cream" turned out to be Crisco. The laughter echoed as we compared skin tones. For the first time, I audibly heard my family's acceptance of how I looked. The truth is they had always accepted me regardless of my skin color. My family knelt down, locked eyes with me, and said, "Camey, you're beautiful just the way you are." From that day on, I never applied Crisco (or anything else, for that matter) in an attempt to change my skin color.

This acceptance, however, didn't instantly heal the scars of rejection. I still had to battle the fear of others who saw me as different from the rest of my family. My mission became about proving to others that I was, in fact, accepted. Not only was I accepted, but chosen!

KINDERGARTEN

When I was old enough to attend school, I embraced the role of the class clown, always eager to bring laughter to my peers. Although academic success was important, I didn't consistently rank at the top of my class. I had feelings of disappointment and, as a result, resorted to humor as a coping mechanism. Unfortunately, I bought into the misconception that being funny required sacrificing self-respect and occasionally appearing foolish. Despite maintaining this comedic facade, internally, I started grappling with severe anxiety. This anxiety led to stomach ulcers which worsened when I was faced with the prospect of being called on without the correct answer or, even worse—having to write on the chalkboard. I started striving for perfectionism in order to hide my flaws.

Despite my insecurities and fear of judgment or criticism, I did find acceptance and admiration from most of my peers. Then we faced the unexpected departure of our second-grade teacher. Surprisingly, my dad, or Mr. Thompson, as the students called him, became her replacement. Initially apprehensive, this change became a welcomed surprise. I soon discovered the joy his teaching style brought to the classroom. His fairness and fun-loving nature not only endeared him to the students but also made me appreciate having him as my protector. The absence of bullies for the rest of the year was no doubt the result of Dad's presence, the respect he commanded, and more importantly, my own kind and humorous demeanor.

For the most part, my young elementary experience was enjoyable, despite facing challenges like surgery. Upon returning to school after a particular surgery, I discovered a fascinating art project displayed atop the room. Dad helped kids create their own facial profiles, and since mine wasn't there, I asked my dad if I could make one. Promptly, he offered to help me create one. Over the weekend, he used a projector to cast my shadow onto colored paper, then I meticulously cut out the drawn silhouette, and he pasted it alongside the others. However, upon seeing my profile, I was shocked. It resembled the witch from The Wizard of Oz, complete with an underbite. I had never seen my profile before. Suddenly I felt mortified. I tried to remember why I wanted that profile picture taken in the first place. How could I make that picture disappear without being noticed? I knew leaving my profile posted on the classroom wall was just not going to be an option.

I was ashamed to admit I was grappling with so many emotions. I tried to convince my dad I didn't need to share the profile picture. While I danced around the topic to avoid embarrassment, Dad was trying to reassure me of my beauty. However, what I perceived was not the same as what my dad was saying. The scar of warped self-perception, on display for my peers to see, became etched in my heart that day.

THE WOUND

Venturing beyond our small town of Roanoke was always an adventure, especially when visiting a restaurant called Pancho's. In the 1980s, Pancho's, a glorified Mexican buffet, was a personal favorite. There was a small Mexican flag on every table, and raising it got the attention of the wait staff to bring anything your heart desired. A favorite treat was the warm sopapillas covered in cinnamon and sugar.

I would generously apply an ample portion of honey, making the sopapillas the undeniable highlight of those outings. One day while standing in line and trying to contain my excitement, I saw an older man smiling at me, but then I realized he was laughing at me, nudging his wife to look at me as well. For a brief moment, I couldn't imagine why this man would be talking about me. As we approached the place to pick up our trays, I instinctively followed my dad's example and started to hand the man a tray. He looked at me, laughed, and said with a mocking tone, "Look at you . . . you little retarded troll girl." He then turned to his wife and continued to discuss me further before dismissively telling me not to touch his tray as he grabbed his own. I was silenced by overwhelming emotions. Embarrassed and hurt, tears began puddling in the corner of my eyes. Holding back my tears, I followed my dad and sat down. The man deliberately positioned himself so he could continue to pester me from a distance. I didn't want my parents to notice his glares toward me, so I responded to his rude stares with equal intensity, meeting him with mean looks in return. It was at that moment that I made an inner vow that I was justified and had every right to put this man in his place. And anyone else who might make fun of me in the future.

This encounter left another scar on my heart. Even though I later tried to explain to my parents that a grown man was making fun of me, I couldn't articulate the depths of my emotions at such a young age. I subsequently threw a cloak over myself, instinctively wanting to hide from the possibility of being rejected. In response, I started to react aggressively toward those who caused me to feel that way. It was a defense mechanism that originally came from a heart full of purity and innocence that had been overwhelmed with shame and embarrassment. Additionally, I developed a sense of self-righteousness and a sense of justice, and I began to tell myself that I was better than others, capable of perceiving wrong for what it was.

EMOTIONAL DAMAGE

In the intricate dance of life, it became evident that God's hand was undeniably orchestrating my journey forward. However, this certainly did not eliminate the harshness of the world. It felt as if an unseen bullseye had been affixed to me, drawing the aim of others who sought to hit their mark. At the same time God was calling, I began to act out. I would become intensely angry because I lived in fear of being wounded. Because of failed attempts to express myself clearly and articulately—I was, in fact, often unheard due to my speech articulation—my frustrations boiled over. I would resort to either silence, stuffing my frustration, or at other times, yelling, hoping that would miraculously enable me to be heard. After these episodes, I would feel a sense of shame for not expressing emotions in a more appropriate way, which obviously would have been the better choice. Sometimes it seemed like I was on a seesaw going from one extreme to another; however, I predominately preferred to live in joy.

    One memory stands out in our Roanoke home—a moment when frustration got the upper hand, and because I wasn't able to articulate my frustration, I ended up yelling. It was one of those times when something or someone had just gotten on my nerves; I'm not certain what triggered it. Suddenly, my emotions went from zero to one hundred. As I tried to express my frustration, my mom or one of my sisters found it amusing and started laughing. Their laughter added to my irritation because again I felt like I was being mocked. Fueled by frustration, I went up the stairs, intentionally making the most racket possible by stomping and banging with a baton along the way. I wanted everyone to know I was upset, although, by that time, my whole family was fully aware.

Upon reaching the bedroom, despite being short, I impulsively rearranged all my furniture to block the door to create a barrier. In a fit of anger, I even constructed a makeshift staircase. Climbing up on the dresser that had been pushed over to the intercom, I shouted something like, "I am so mad at you! You make me so mad. I hate you. I won't eat anything, and I'm going to call CPS on you." Looking back, I now realize I was being a brat and threatening to withhold eating as a way to punish them would only punish myself. How I knew about CPS at that age is still a mystery.

My tantrum came to a quick end when I heard my dad's footsteps on the stairs. He knocked on the door and tried to open it, but it was locked. He then firmly said, "Camey, you need to open the door right now." I knew I was in trouble because whenever my dad disciplined me, he meant business. Quickly, I unlocked the door, scrambling to remove all the furniture before he opened it.

Following Dad's stern warning, I realized I needed to get my act together and was embarrassed for how I'd acted. I wanted to honor my threat of not eating but the savory aroma of dinner tempted my senses and made my stomach growl in protest. Unable to resist temptation, I slowly walked down the stairs clutching my blanket with puppy eyes that begged for mercy while silently pleading for food. I wasn't met with rejection or any reprimands concerning my behavior; nevertheless, an unspoken acknowledgment lingered in the air—obviously, I had been in the wrong.

A couple of days slipped by after that emotional outburst. My mom approached me, and with a gentle touch, she cradled my small face in her hands. Then lovingly, she said, "Camey, I need to discuss something very important with you. If you were ever to call CPS, they would likely come and take you away." Tears welled up in her eyes, "Then we might not be able to ever get you back. You must never say such things or even consider it, even when you're upset."

Deeply remorseful for my previous words and actions, a heavy sense of guilt washed over me for betraying those who loved me the most. I vowed never to speak this way again even when upset, and thankfully, I never did.

MY "LITTLE BLACK BOOK"

To help me cope with my feelings, Mom gave me a little locked red journal where I could record my thoughts and emotions. I kept the keys hidden in a secret spot to ensure no one could unlock it and read the private thoughts penned in that journal. However, I kept the keys in such a secretive place that often I would lose track of their location!

The journal turned into something different than my mom intended. When starting to navigate friendships, I quickly learned the difference between safe people and unsafe people. The safe people were typically the children who would notice my scars and ask about them directly. They might say, "Hey, why do you have scars on your lip?" or "What happened? Were you in an accident?" I appreciated their direct honesty and curiosity because, after I explained my facial scars, they would often take a moment to process, and then, more often than not, invite me to join in their play.

It was the adults who had a much more difficult time processing or accepting my appearance. They seemed to assume that my having a speech impediment also meant I lacked intelligence.

I never fully understood the deep impact that encounters such as the one I had at Pancho's had on my life until I grew older. Years of trying to hide this scar only resulted in my heart becoming more hardened, whenever I felt threatened or ashamed. It was difficult when I was singled out or humiliated in public. I would seek to balance the scales of justice by giving similar treatment or lashing out in hurtful ways in order for my voice to be heard.

I knew the Bible told us to never keep records of wrongs, but I found it challenging to adhere to that principle. During that time, I struggled to recall specific details about things that happened, especially the "whys." Perhaps my forgetfulness stemmed from trauma, the effects of anesthesia from multiple surgeries, or an undiagnosed attention deficit. The bottom line was I would easily forget why people had wronged me, and felt compelled to keep a record for self-protection, so I could hold onto resentment, as I felt that was all I had left . . . my resentment. Resentment not only became a coping mechanism, but it was also the only thing I felt I could control. Consequently, I chose to hold onto it.

Despite my worry about forgetting, if a subject captured my interest or held significance, I could effortlessly remember it. Conversely, if something didn't capture my interest, it would slip from memory as though it was never there. While this trait could have worked in my favor by preventing the harboring of grudges, I desired to remember why I was upset so that I could safeguard myself from this pain again or nurture resentment. In hindsight, this inclination was highly detrimental.

In many aspects of life, God has consistently revealed His goodness toward me despite my tendency toward self-destruction. In fact, the entries in this red journal were not all negative. One entry was a specific list of the exact things I desired in the man I would one day marry: He had to be taller than six feet with blond hair and blue eyes and had to be able to sing, and of course, above all, he had to love the Lord with all his heart. Even though I don't know why I wrote this list when I was young, God did answer my prayers—specifically. Oh, and despite it being red, everyone else in my family still refers to the journal as my "little black book."

While it's true, no person should ever be made to feel less worthy or shamed in any way, much less a young child by a grown adult, learning the power of forgiveness would eventually allow me to confront this wound as Jesus commanded. Forgiveness helped me address my scars of shame and rejection.

CHAPTER SEVEN
Finding My Voice

God's plan was at work even as each setback became a setup for the next chapter of my life. Heal the Children's ministry generously covered the costs of my initial surgeries, setting the stage for my recovery.

In June 1985, a pivotal moment unfolded in my family's history, shaping our story in unexpected ways. Dad was called by God to this small town outside Fort Worth to start a nondenominational church called Cornerstone Community Church. For the first few months, the church met in the lobby of Northwest Bank. After an initial period, it was relocated across the street in a strip mall for the next seven years. My parents constructed a custom country, saltbox-shaped home with dark red bricks (the one with the intercom). This house was only the second one built in the newly developed rural subdivision called Brookstone. Brookstone lay just outside the heart of Roanoke, surrounded by hills, rock piles, snakes, and refreshing clean air. The house featured a large pond in the front that was connected to a spillway leading to another pond in the back. We had two neighbors, and one of our closest neighbors was none other than Byron Nelson, the famous golfer, located a mile away at the entrance of Brookstone.

Brookstone became my sanctuary, a place where I captured my youngest memories, my heart sang, and wild imagination roamed freely. On many clear nights, I would lie on our trampoline under the big Texas night sky, captured by the brilliant stars above. In those moments, I found myself immersed in contemplation, reflecting on life and my hopes and dreams. My deep affection for animals was evident as I had a knack for winning over the most skittish creatures, often becoming friends and teaching them tricks. Some might say I was a bit of a tomboy, always running around barefoot, playing competitive games, trying to outrun the boys, getting my hands dirty by uncovering worms, whipping up mud pies, and scaling tall trees to the very top. Yet, I had another side with a fondness for makeup, twirly skirts, and playing with Barbie dolls.

If I wasn't outside or playing "office" inside, you could find me watching the same movie over and over hundreds of times. The Little Mermaid was one of these timeless classics for me. Because of that one movie alone, my parents knew there was nothing wrong with my brain as I was able to recite every word to every single line in that movie. I might not remember what I studied for a test at school, but I quite literally had the entire movie memorized. The theme of The Little Mermaid for me was to belong, and my heart wanted to fit in just like Ariel wanted legs.

During this part of my childhood, I was fortunate to be blessed with the gift of friendship from two special individuals,

Lyndee and Andrew, from our church in Roanoke. They knew me not as the girl with scars on my face or a girl with different-colored skin, but simply as C.J. Their love knew no bounds and came without demands. Together, we loved, laughed until we cried (or in my case, peed my pants), fought with all our might, and cried together through good times and bad. Most importantly, we had a deep love for one another. With them, I could take off the "cloak of protection" I wore because, with them, I was safe.

We spent much of our time together outdoors and I was the most afraid of bugs—let's get real, terrified of any bug, period. I didn't want to let my friends in on that little secret, although I'm almost certain they knew. Andrew had a knack for catching slimy large frogs, and sometimes they would surprise us by releasing their bladder. Laughter filled the air as we giggled uncontrollably. Although initially frightened by the frogs, I enjoyed every minute playing together. We caught crickets and organized races for them. We released them to see who would reach the finish line through our obstacle course. Occasionally, the crickets would be a bit sluggish, so we'd use our fingers to gently nudge them, providing some motivation to get them moving. Usually that little tactic did the trick.

Another vivid memory revolved around the time we stumbled upon several unopened bottles of beer, just a block away in an empty cul-de-sac. For fun, Andrew and I decided to toss the beer bottles toward a rock pile, and we had an absolute blast. That is, until a skunk appeared! In a selfless act, Andrew shielded me, and thankfully, we didn't get sprayed. The laughter and pure-hearted fun of innocent children filled that moment. Andrew and I watched another favorite animated movie classic, Robin Hood, which was on repeat because it held such a special place in my heart. Robin loved Maid Marian and was not only willing to fight for others in the pursuit of justice but also for the love and affection of his lady.

Perhaps the childhood memory that still means the most to me was the day Andrew and I made a pact that we were going to be each other's "backups," you know, if we couldn't find a spouse by a certain age. We promised we'd be there for each other, even spitting on it to seal the deal with a firm handshake. I was grateful that the pressure of trying to find a spouse was lifted from my shoulders at such a young age, since I didn't believe anyone would really want to marry me.

TRIUMPHS

In the world of backyard adventures and childhood triumphs, Chad, Lyndee's older brother, stood out because he was kind, charming, and compassionate. Despite his captivating presence, I managed to keep my composure around him—or at least, that's what I'd like to believe. Our families shared countless memories together from our church, and they became like our extended family. Back when I was a struggling seven-year-old trying to conquer the art of swimming, my mom, ever the advocate of conquering fears, insisted on enrolling me in swimming lessons. However, my traumatic encounter with the anesthesia mask had instilled in me a paralyzing fear of anything covering my face, which especially included submerging my face under water.

Despite a few attempts at the Trophy Club pool, I found myself panicking and fleeing the water, rendering conventional swim lessons impossible. Then, on a sunny day with only a handful of pool-goers, Mom's eyes lit up as she spotted Chad. Seizing the moment, she excitedly proposed to me that Chad could be my swimming teacher.

There were many times when Chad had kindly come to my aid in their pool—guiding me to the edge or offering a piggyback ride. I reluctantly agreed that only Chad could take on the role of being my swimming instructor. Glancing back at my mom, I saw that through a series of sign language cues she clarified to Chad the need for me to put my head under water.

As I mentioned, all my previous swim lessons had ended with me ultimately succumbing to defeat. However, Chad convinced me to lie on a blue mat blowing bubbles in the water while kicking my legs. By the time I realized it, he had carried me to a depth where I no longer could touch the bottom. His comforting words were, "I've got you, Camey. You've made it this far. Don't quit. You can do it." Initially indifferent to the exercise, I found myself willing to endure anything for Chad's sake.

The lesson may have been cut slightly short; I had done my best and ran to seek refuge with my mom. But that day was a milestone for me, since Chad had instilled in me the confidence to submerge my face. His extraordinary patience became the cornerstone of my aquatic adventures, transforming swimming lessons into a journey of trust, encouragement, and ultimately, triumph. It was a win, and another fear was conquered!

BUMS

Growing up in the Thompson family was a unique and beautiful experience. My parents excelled in doing things beautifully. As a pastor's kid (PK for short), I was used to them always inviting people over. Mom would cook for our family and often for our church; my parents considered it an honor to invite others and serve them. Mom, a decorator, had the table beautifully set and decorated with ironed cloth napkins and flowers picked from outside. Known for her open heart and open doors, she welcomed anyone without hesitation. As a result, I grew up embracing the concept of knowing no strangers. Our home had an inviting atmosphere; the doors were never locked, and often it felt like a revolving door that brought in people from various walks of life.

Dad's commitment to serving others, even a homeless shelter under a bridge in Fort Worth, added a compassionate touch to our family dynamics. The leader of the shelter would occasionally drop off someone in need at our front door. I recall a particularly remarkable moment when Mom shared a memory. She was seated in the balcony at a conference in downtown Fort Worth. From her vantage point, she observed a man entering and taking a seat. It was evident to her that he was homeless, and throughout the evening, she felt a strong prompting from the Lord concerning him. Taking the initiative, she approached him and introduced herself as Judi. He shook her hand and said, "Hi, I am Tony." In that instant, she said, "Tony, I believe you're meant to come and live with our family." When she brought Tony home, Dad was not upset by her actions because she would have never done such a thing without clear direction from

God. Dad recognized her obedience to the Lord, and this collaborative effort between my parents showcased their teamwork. This was indicative of the normalcy with which they handled every situation, almost always in agreement.

Tony, a man with few teeth, wore only overalls and kept a red handkerchief in his back pocket. He quickly integrated into our family. He wore his smile well with what few teeth he had and, over the course of a month, adapted to our family's rhythm. We enjoyed laughter, playing games, fellowship, and sharing home-cooked meals. He even showed us his magic tricks, stuffing his red handkerchief into his thumb and making it disappear, a game that never failed to bring me joy, and I was constantly trying to learn the secrets to his tricks.

Tony's presence was a constant for two months, and then, one day, as fast as he came into our lives, he was gone. I often inquired where my friend went, but Dad told me enduringly and with sadness in his eyes, "Tony chose to go back to his home." Tony's decision did not settle well with my brother Tyler, who asked, "Why would he leave us when he had a family here who loved him?" It was sometime later that I learned Tony lived under a bridge in Fort Worth. I would ask from time to time, "Where's Tony?" but I saw the hurt in my family's eyes each time I asked, so I learned not to pry further, as it was hard to let go of someone's destructive choices. We all cared deeply for him. Even though that was a hard experience, I learned the importance of loving people deeply yet loosely, since we can't control other peoples' decisions, even when they are destructive.

After Tony left, other individuals, mostly men, came through our doors. Some stayed briefly, while others became more extended members of our family much like Tony. Despite their diverse backgrounds, I never felt fearful of these men. Instead, I felt joyful whenever a new person came to share our table.

Jim, another visitor, wore overalls like Tony yet he was quieter and less outgoing. Even as a young girl, I developed a sense of knowing how to meet people where they were emotionally and spiritually. One day, I saw Jim fishing for crawdads in the pond behind our house. Despite my initial aversion to bugs or fish, I wanted to join him, since I had seen Tyler bring buckets of them home in the past. I knew when my presence was welcomed, and I knew when it had been overstayed. One day, I walked down to the edge of the pond behind our house and sat next to Jim.

"Jim, can I crawdad fish with you?"

Without a word, he looked at me as if he were debating his next move. He looked away for some time, then turned and handed me a pole, showing me how to use it only once. I knew not to ask any further questions, as that might change his mind about letting me join him on his fishing excursion. I extended the pole, but mine didn't go nearly as far out as Jim's. I'm not sure exactly how long we spent fishing for crawdads, but Mom said it was hours and hours as she watched us from the kitchen window. I caught only one crawdad that day. This was the only time I saw Jim smile. I'm not sure who benefited more from that moment in time—me, learning how to crawdad fish, or Jim, being able to sit with me sharing only a few words. I never did learn his story. Was he hurt as a little boy? Did he ever have a child, or perhaps a little girl, my age? What I know about that day is Jim and I shared a peaceful moment together and, more importantly, it was a healing one.

If I wasn't at home, you could often find me immersing myself in activities at our Cornerstone Community Church. There I would engage in self-entertainment for hours at a time as I tucked myself away in a closet. I would be engrossed in playing office with my assortment of makeshift paper scraps. Given that my siblings were significantly older and a few had moved out by this time, I basically became an only child, so I was adept at entertaining myself.

Two specific elements endeared themselves to me during my time at church—music and communion. Each provided a chance for me to feel "extra" holy. I was aware of the boundaries regarding what I could touch and do, so I would watch my dad take the leftover bread and juice from communion to the kitchen and arrange them on a perfectly ironed, starched, white tablecloth my mom had prepared. Having to stay up late after church was commonplace, so hunger struck often, and much to my mom's amusement, I would devour two bites of food and declare myself stuffed. One Sunday, unable to wait any longer to eat, I spotted the remnants of bread and juice on the glowing white table, and I couldn't resist. I succumbed to temptation, grabbed them and made a quick retreat to a makeshift fort beneath the table, surrounded by the tablecloth ironed linen. I'm quite certain I consumed it all, and experienced both an extra anointing and an extra stomachache that day. Despite the occasional discomfort, communion days remained my favorite church observance.

Thanks to my dad's penchant for staying on the cutting-edge of worship, music played a significant role at Cornerstone. Dad delighted in exploring new sounds of worship, embracing artists such as Integrity Worship, Maranatha, and the Gaithers, which included Psalty. The church didn't have hymnals but utilized a projection screen. The musical experience was exceptional, thanks to both my dad's appreciation and the beloved Arnold family. Their phenomenal voices, harmonies, and original songs resonated throughout the sanctuary.

Carol Arnold, in particular, would occasionally invite me to join them on stage to lead the congregation in worship. I was not one to refuse, as I was outgoing and always willing to take an opportunity to be seen. Despite not having vocal lessons at this time, I always knew how to offer a heartfelt song of praise to the Lord.

WILDA

One Sunday afternoon, as I was walking in our church, I heard an angelic sound coming from behind the doors of the sanctuary, a sound I'd never heard before. It was as though there was a force pulling me inside. Slowly peering through the cracked door, I saw an older woman standing behind a keyboard worshiping from the depths of her soul. It was the most beautiful sound, and it shook me to my core. Her name was Wilda, and she was preparing for her concert later in the evening service. After her concert, which felt more like a time of heavenly ministry, Mom asked if Wilda could pray for me. I was so excited because that's what I'd been praying for. Mom mentioned to Wilda that I loved to sing, although Wilda had only heard me speak. Many people, including powerful individuals who came through our church, had prayed for me before. However, when Wilda laid her hand on my head, something shifted in my body and spirit. She asked me to lift my hands as she anointed my head with oil, and she began to speak and prophesy over the present and into my future.

"Sister, I anoint you with oil as I call forth a voice that will resonate throughout the nations. You are called to all parts of the world, including Asia, Mexico, Australia, Singapore, South America, and throughout the land. A voice that tells of God's goodness and faithfulness. A voice that will call nations back to Him, a voice that will shake the land." She moved her hand, placed it on my abdomen, and said in a firm voice filled with authority, "I call out a sound!" Just then, I doubled over as if someone had gut-punched me, although nothing physically hurt. I knew something in my body and soul had shifted. My eyes were closed, but I could feel the room getting brighter, and I knew that the presence of God and His angels were in the room. It's difficult to articulate the exact feelings I had at that moment, but I felt the same warmth and peaceful sensation I had felt as a six-year-old at the New Orleans Healing Conference. I could see the same bright light I saw when being baptized and the same peace I felt while sitting in the back seat of the car talking to Jesus as we drove to Houston—it was Him!

    Mom asked if I would like to take voice lessons from Wilda, and I could only muster enough to nod in agreement because I was left speechless from her prayer. Days later, as we approached Wilda's home, I could see that we were not in Roanoke anymore.

The houses were mostly older, smaller white wooden frames with a few bright yellow, green, and purple homes sporadically sprinkled throughout. Black metal bars adorned the windows and black wrought-iron fences guarded the steps to the entry of most of the homes. I gulped. The notion of voice lessons started to lose its appeal. "Mom, this is so far away. I'm tired. Can we go back home? How much longer?" Mom responded, "We are almost there, and aren't these beautiful, historical homes?" I couldn't quite tell who she was trying to convince because, at that point, I was afraid and started wondering if I'd even make it to my next birthday!

We arrived at Wilda's quaint, all-white wooden home and walked up the stairs to the front door. As Wilda opened the door and peered through the screen door, she greeted us with a great big smile, like Octavia Spencer from the movie The Help. We walked into the entryway, and there was a gas fireplace that looked like a stove that kept the house cozy and warm. She excused herself for a minute, went into another room, and pulled out her older keyboard. I heard her say, in her deep southern accent, "Camey, you can come with me dear." I typically kept a close eye on my mom, but this time, I wasn't sure where she'd gone in the house; however, I knew I would be safe in the presence of Wilda.

As I approached Wilda, she effortlessly played chords on her keyboard while starting up a casual conversation. Curious, she asked about my favorite song. With confidence, I replied, "Amazing Grace."

"Alright, child, stand up straight and move right here in front of me. Let's hear it," she instructed. With a full voice, I belted out "Amazing Grace," in the arrangement of Amy Grant, one of my favorite singers at the time. Just before reaching one of the big notes, she interrupted. Disappointment clouded my expression. I had hoped to showcase my vocal range and power.

She inquired about my singing aspirations, and in a soft voice, I murmured, "Ahhh . . . Amy Grant . . . Sandi Patti . . ." But before I could finish, she halted me mid-sentence. Kneeling down to my level, eye to eye, she emphatically declared, "Girl, you aren't going to sing like no white girl. Girl, you are going to sing with some soul."

She continued, "Now I want you to sing "Amazing Grace" from the top." Hitting some full minor chords, she set the stage for me to begin. But just as before, she cut me off—even earlier in the song this time. Placing her hand on my diaphragm, she said, "Girl, sing from your gut, sister. Sing it like you mean it. Sing it like you know what "Amazing Grace" is. Where did "Amazing Grace" come from? Who is "Amazing Grace?" Camey, are you amazed at God's goodness in your life? Are you grateful for where you've been and where God is taking you?"

Standing there speechless, I closed my eyes for a moment and quickly asked God, "God, am I truly grateful? Do I know the meaning of "Amazing Grace?" If not, God, show me, teach me."

She said, "Let's start over," and from the billowing of my soul, a sound formed that was brand new to me. It was a sound that was deep and full of soul straight from a place I didn't know existed. I started, "A . . . A . . . AAAAmazing Grace, how sweet the sound." As I was singing, I saw Mom's eyes open wide, and Wilda's eyes filled with tears, along with a slow smile as she said, "There it is .

. . That's it, that's it! Now, that, my child, is the sound of "Amazing Grace!"' This was the making of another core memory and a life-changing moment. It was a sound that came from my soul, one that filled the room and shifted the atmosphere. It was a God-given sound like she prophesied would one day shake the nations. From that day forward, I decided I did not want to sing like a white girl, but I wanted soul, like Whitney Houston. My sound did not always come from the best trills, but from the cry of my heart. That day, I became not just a singer, but a worshipper with a new sound.

I don't remember taking many more lessons from Wilda because she moved away. But I am so grateful to God for bringing her into my life. Meeting her was a crucial turning point, as she carried a key to unlock my God-given calling.

GAME TIME

Not long after meeting Wilda, I decided to broaden my singing horizons beyond the confines of the church. An invitation led me to perform at an event held at the local baseball fields. I opted to sing "Amazing Grace," which I had worked on with Wilda. I felt a twinge of nervousness as I took the stage.

The setting was intimate, with only a handful of people around, mostly familiar faces that heightened my anxiety. However, as my name was called and I approached the microphone, the background noise of men playing baseball faded. As I started singing a cappella, the world around me vanished; I could only hear the echo of my voice. Nothing else mattered as I poured my heart into the song, grateful to the One who had given me His amazing grace.

As I hit the last note and sang the final word, silence filled the air. After what felt like an eternity, the fields erupted in a thunderous roar. At the time, I didn't dwell much on it, but my dad later revealed that everyone had stopped playing as the games were in progress just to hear me. The realization that my voice had captivated an entire audience brought more of a confirmation of the call upon my life. It was not just my voice, but His gift to me.

CHAPTER EIGHT
Resurrecting the Dead

A setback occurred in 1987 when my parents' insurance refused coverage for a crucial procedure deemed essential for ongoing cleft palate reconstruction. They had to wait two years for insurance approval. At that point, confronted with what seemed like an overwhelming obstacle, they did what they could and turned to a teaching hospital in Chicago that provided free surgeries.

As I entered a conference room, I scanned the surroundings. A noticeable chill covered the space, sending a shiver through me. A man with an unfriendly tone instructed me to take a seat in a small chair positioned smack in the center of this cold room. I felt like the newest attraction at the local zoo, as "spectators" began talking about me while peering through a glass window as though I couldn't hear them. The panel, composed of doctors, nurses, a speech therapist, an anesthesiologist, student interns, a patient care coordinator, and a few men in red hats sat in a semicircle around a raised desk, affording them the best view.

I sat upright with my hands discreetly tucked under my legs, maintaining eye contact with everyone. Occasionally my eyes darted to the side, keeping an eye on where my dad was standing. At times, it felt like I could sense the panel's hesitance. Their faces were rigid and emotionless, without even the slightest hint of a smile. While sitting and observing what I mentally labeled the "death panel," I recognized the importance of being cooperative and pleasant. It felt like an audition where I sought to secure a role without fully understanding all the details. Perhaps another surgery at worst.

One by one, individuals began to descend from the panel to closely examine me. Each person declared their findings to the rest of the group, while the others took notes. A man in a white coat approached, and I made an effort to sit still, casting sidelong glances at him as if anticipating an imminent injection with a big, long needle. Dad reassured me repeatedly before walking into the room that I wouldn't receive a shot without prior notice, offering little comfort to my internal anxiety. The doctor instructed me to open my mouth wide, stick out my tongue, and say, "Ahh." Peering into my mouth with a light, he exclaimed, "Oh wow, yes, I see," then paused for a moment before stating, "Her case is extremely complex." From his expressions, I gathered that if he considered the challenge too complicated, possibly the entire panel might find me or my case too difficult to address.

They requested that my parents take me out of the room so they could discuss the case privately. During this brief interlude, I took the opportunity to play on the indoor playground, seeking to alleviate the tension that had built up inside, afraid to let it outwardly show. Shortly afterward, they invited us to rejoin them in the room, and the spokesperson of the group turned to my dad, and replied, "Mr. Thompson, you have a fine, well-behaved daughter, but her case is remarkably complex, something we don't typically encounter. I'm not entirely sure she would fit the usual profile for our surgical team."

A moment of silence hung in the air before he continued, "However, the majority of our medical team has decided to give this surgery a try. But I must be candid, there is a lack of optimism, as we doubt she will have improvement in her speech or be able to speak clearly. Immediate placement of tubes in her ears is crucial along with continued speech therapy." What the doctors did not know was that my singing voice was miraculously much clearer than my speaking voice.

My "audition" was successful as I secured the role and got the part. The doctors agreed to do the next surgery. The only problem was, I did not get the role I actually wanted, which would have been no surgery at all.

Despite the pessimistic comments from doctors, my parents adamantly refused to accept their proclamations that would silence my dreams. My parents were resolute in putting a stop to the curses that seemed to be coming my way, and Dad, although kind in his words, challenged the doctor's prognosis. Dad informed one of the many doctors about my talent and passion for singing. However, even before those words could fully escape his lips, they were met with an immediate, firm "No! She will likely never sing." It was clear that the medical professionals did not want to entertain any unrealistic expectations or wishful thinking regarding my singing aspirations. My parents recognized not only my interest but also my skill, which confirmed what God had told me. They desired to do their part by providing vocal, piano, and speech lessons to nurture my gifts while also instilling confidence. I am full of gratitude to my parents who chose to speak life and words of encouragement over me. They trusted and believed what the Lord said would come true, regardless of contradictory opinions from doctors, who had never heard me sing so they weren't aware of my gift.

Although teaching hospitals are amazing for training purposes, they left me feeling much like a specimen in an experiment. Words were spoken to predict death to my dreams resulting in scars that God was able to use in a remarkable way to teach me resilience and determination. This was a catalyst to embrace His truth rather than man's. From the perspective of where I stand now, I am grateful for the many surgeries, and the privilege of living in America, which provided access to wonderful medical care. I understand now that the "death panel" of doctors weren't trying to be "dream crushers" or intentionally rob me of opportunities; they were merely stating facts. They assessed, observed, and spoke their medical understanding of what they perceived to be true. What appeared at the time to be the possible death of a dream was, in fact, a setup for God to resurrect His calling by miraculously denying their truth over me and giving me His truth.

THE RESCUE

I not only was a big daydreamer but also experienced vivid dreams while sleeping. One night, I found myself dreaming that I was within the confines of a deep, round circular pit. Thankfully, a ladder in the pit offered a glimmer of hope. With optimism, I secured the ladder and believed my escape was within my reach. I ascended, and then the reality of the dream shifted. Perched on the top step of the ladder, close to my escape, I discovered I was too short to climb out of the pit. Persistent efforts proved futile, and I grappled with a sense of defeat. Determined, I made one last attempt, teetering on the top step of the ladder, and a plea for help escaped my lips. I could hear footsteps, and suddenly, a man's strong, yet familiar arm, reached down and grabbed mine—pulling me to safety and rescuing me from this pit.

Not fully comprehending the significance of this dream, it remained a vivid memory. I can see that God was preparing me for what was to come—His provision for my future.

~

Although my parents were extremely grateful for the care and surgery I received in Chicago, a lingering dissatisfaction remained. Travel from Texas to Chicago usually took two days, accompanied by many expenses. Additionally, my continued surgeries had not been approved by the panel, so continuing to make these trips didn't guarantee success. The feeling of concern that the doctors were using me mainly for training purposes, diminishing me to a "case number" rather than by my actual name, did not breed confidence in the best treatment possible. It was time to try to find a new source of care.

During this treatment period, Mom discovered the Baylor School of Dentistry in Dallas, where people could undergo usual dental procedures or removal of wisdom teeth. These procedures were performed by students in their last semester under strict supervision by an expert dentist, all at a substantial discount. This discovery presented a win-win situation for my family, especially considering our lack of dental insurance.

Upon arrival at Baylor, Mom inquired if any doctors specialized in craniofacial issues, specifically cleft lip and palate. After encountering confused stares, we were met with multiple negative responses. However, God's intervention in my life occurred when Dr. Cheryl Anderson-Cermin overheard someone asking, and she humbly replied, "I have worked with cleft palates; I can take a look at her." Later, we discovered that she was among the leading craniofacial orthodontists in her field, well-renowned and well-loved. She specialized in tackling some of the toughest challenges in pediatric craniofacial deformities in dentistry and orthodontics, particularly focusing on cleft lip and palate. Yet, at that moment, we had no idea about the remarkable woman we were about to meet. The day was hectic, yet Dr. Anderson-Cermin took time in her schedule to look at me. She and my mom immediately connected, sharing a kindred spirit. After she laid me back in the dental chair, I felt like I was the only person in her world. She looked directly into my eyes with a sincere gaze, inquiring about my thoughts and concerns. Following the examination, she swiftly declared, "I know the perfect cranial plastic surgeon for Camey. He's the best in Dallas. Truthfully, he's one of the best in the world, and we've worked together on multiple surgeries. He has a wonderful heart— I just know this will be a good fit."

How could I have known that the broken roads of countless surgeons and hospitals would lead straight to this moment, forever altering the course of my medical history? Just a week later, I sat on an examination table in a room, accompanied by my dad and mom. In the corridor, I could hear the shuffle of papers that signaled the presence of Dr. Hobar and Mary Breen, the nurse coordinator, reviewing my chart. A swift knock announced the entrance of Dr. Hobar and with him came an undeniable shift in the atmosphere.

His presence radiated kindness, love, and a humble confidence that carried a profound weight with every word he uttered. "Camey!" His face lit up with a warm smile as he looked directly into my eyes. I could feel his heartbeat of love as he said, "I've heard so many wonderful things from Dr. Anderson-Cermin, and I am thrilled to meet you." Turning to my parents, he greeted them with the same enthusiasm and respect he had bestowed upon me.

Dr. Hobar swiftly conducted a brief assessment, asking me to open my mouth wide and having me tilt my head back while he peered in with his light and tongue depressor. He kindly asked me to say "ahh," and his gentle demeanor and positive words filled me with reassurance. Articulating clear, realistic plans of action, he commanded the room with authority, ensuring that his team was aligned with the correct path ahead.

Dr. Hobar encouraged questions from me and my parents as he addressed each one with a collaborative spirit. Each response was accompanied by a thorough and precise explanation. Dr. Hobar's approach made us all feel included, granting us a clear understanding of the plan that lay ahead.

God surrounded me with a team of angels in the form of doctors, Dr. Anderson-Cermin and Dr. Hobar, who worked hand in hand and blazed the trail for me not just to live, but to thrive. A multidisciplinary team of experts including ear, nose, and throat specialists; plastic surgeons; oral surgeons; speech pathologists; audiologists; orthodontists; psychologists; and social workers joined Drs. Hobar and Anderson-Cermin. These caring and skilled professionals remained my doctors until the completion of my care. They were more than mere medical professionals; they became an integral part of my life. They were my heroes wearing scrubs instead of capes, cheerleaders in life who spoke words of life, instead of death, into and over me. Being in their presence was always something I looked forward to, as I felt not only loved but safe. I trusted them with every fiber of my being. They became the miracle in my life, advocating for my voice, dreams, aspirations, and even financially gifting most of my medical care and surgeries. They performed delicate surgeries that enabled me not just to speak clearly but allowed me the ability to continue to sing. With their help, I became the overcomer I was called to be.

Reflecting on my earlier dream, I can see now the strong arm that reached down into the pit and gently grabbed hold of me. The hand felt oddly familiar. The man's eyes that radiated tenderness, the same loving eyes I had come to cherish and adore, I realized were none other than those of Dr. Hobar. He helped me up out of the pit, embraced me in a tender hug, and simply walked down the road as he was on a mission to rescue me and others like me. I have no doubt that Dr. Hobar and Dr. Anderson-Cermin were sent by God to lift me from the pit of rejection and condemnation, feeling like a shameful outcast, and redeem what the enemy had stolen. They gave me confidence, courage, strength—and my voice. Not only were they an incredibly talented and powerful duo, but they also exemplified a deep love for serving others. Truly they were the hands and feet of Jesus.

CHAPTER NINE

Despite my challenges with articulation at times, the ability to hit notes on key with precision while staying in my chest voice (a fuller deeper sound) came naturally. The piano was my instrument of choice, and the ivory keys weaved their way into the fabric of my soul.

Playing the piano became one of my favorite pastimes as I would hit the piano keys for hours on end. As a toddler, I would stand on tippy toes, and delicately use my fingertips to gently press the keys, creating a beautiful melody of notes. I vividly recall my mother's joy-filled voice saying, "Wow, Camey, that sounds beautiful." I shared her sentiment because regardless of the notes, in my imagination, a full symphony accompanied me as I was playing.

When I sang, a roaring sound would emerge from the depths of my soul, effortlessly shifting the atmosphere around me. I didn't fully grasp the anointing I carried, but I noticed that this sound surfaced only when I engaged in worship. In those moments, my voice became more than just a sound—it became a conduit for something deeper; something beyond mere vocalization.

When I was seven, Mom shared some exciting news with me about an up-and-coming group called TKO, short for Technical Knockout. It was an exclusive platform for talented kids in the Dallas-Fort Worth metroplex, resembling a smaller version of the Disney Club. It was a diverse group composed of talented kids from various walks of life. Each child possessed a unique gift, from exceptional vocal talents to superb dancing and acting skills.

Founded by Marlene Bigley, TKO had a mission to enhance children's confidence and stage presence. Eagerly, I looked forward to experiencing TKO firsthand but wrestled with insecurities and questioned my own abilities and the possibility of not "making the cut."

As we drove to the first audition in Arlington, a blend of excitement and nervousness overwhelmed me. I began overthinking and pondered all the "what ifs": What if the other kids wouldn't accept me? What if they talked about my scars behind my back? What if they didn't like me because of the color of my skin? What if they made fun of the way I spoke—so nasally? What if we were late? Being late could draw unwanted attention from the other kids.

"Oh, Lord, please don't let us be late," I prayed. The "what ifs" weighed heavily on my mind—then, a new emerging anxiety surfaced as I wondered, "Would there be boys in the group?"

In the car, I confided to my mom: "I don't feel so good. I might be sick to my stomach." It wasn't an unusual sensation for me during drives, especially those lasting over fifteen minutes, as I typically needed some food in my belly to avoid such discomfort.

As we drew nearer, a sense of unease settled in—I had a gut feeling that we were lost. "Mom, how much farther do we have?" I asked anxiously.

"I'm not sure, but we should be close," she reassured me. Despite her words, the truth was evident—we were indeed lost. Closing my eyes, I took a deep breath and suggested, "Mom, we don't have to go today. Why don't we just go back home?"

In response, Mom insisted, "Camey, we are almost there. In fact, I can see a church over there. Let me check if that's it."

Feeling the pressure of time, I pleaded, "Mom, it's ten minutes past, and I don't want to be late. Please, Mom, please?"

Mom, determined, pointed out another kid entering the building, exclaiming, "Look, I can see another kid going in. Let's follow her." Sinking deeper into my seat, I relented. I had no other choice, so I reluctantly left the comfort of the car and began walking.

Upon opening the squeaky doors to the gym, I saw that around thirty kids were sitting neatly on the floor in a "crisscross applesauce" style. A TKO helper directed me to my assigned spot, and I was placed in the third row between two kids on a white mark on the floor. My spot was near the front, where everyone would see me, but I quietly sat down.

The girl beside me introduced herself as Keri and whispered, "Hi, nice to meet you. I'm glad you're here." Her warm words were just what was needed at that moment—a friendly face and a reassuring smile. "I'm here," I thought to myself. "Camey, you did it. You made it. This is where you need to be."

Just then, a tall, slender woman, a real-life Barbie doll with her full, beautiful blonde hair and long legs, confidently entered the gym. Addressing us, she exclaimed, "Hi, everyone! I'm so glad you're here today because we are on the precipice of something great. We have a lot to learn, so let's get started." Marlene expressed her passion for seeing others embrace their God-given abilities, expecting nothing less from the group, as she believed we were all made for greatness.

Without wasting time on small talk, Marlene jumped right into the topic of confidence and the importance of owning a room. She instructed each of us to walk to the front, shoulders back, to introduce ourselves by saying our name, age, and one thing of interest. With the microphone held firmly close to her mouth, she set the tone for the session. Impressed by her no-nonsense attitude, I eagerly awaited my turn, inspired by her beauty and confidence.

When it was my turn, I took the microphone with as much poise as I possessed, and confidently said, "Hi, my name is Camey Thompson. I am eight years old, and I love animals and singing." Returning to the designated spot, I listened as applause filled the room—I had successfully completed my first task. My heart was pounding with excitement! My friend Adam from a homeschool group was also present, which made me feel safe. In addition, I met two new girls that day who shared my passion for singing. It became clear this was where I belonged, and these were my people. Even my mom found connections, bonding with another mother who had a son my age. I finally felt like I was home and in a place where my scars were not the object of attention, but that I was being seen for what I had been called to be.

Instantly, a new chapter unfolded—one filled with friends, both guys and girls. These were not like any other kids I had met before. While some were curious about the scars on my face, they all accepted my explanation. The conversations swiftly transitioned after hearing me sing to discussions about my voice—a gift that set me apart. I soon discovered there was more to me than the voice that endeared me to these kids. My outgoing nature, zest for life, and the joy I exuded made me feel welcomed. In this group, I felt safe, which allowed me to let my guard down.

But just like any other performance group, we had to audition for the songs we wanted to sing. In the early days of TKO, our performances were mostly in malls, especially during Christmastime, sometimes three times a day. During each show, we had to get up and introduce ourselves, a practice ingrained in us from day one. My first solo performance was a rendition of, "I Saw Mommy Kissing Santa Claus." Although I enjoyed singing the song, I must admit feeling uneasy singing a song that implied my mom was kissing someone other than her husband (my dad) on Christmas. It took about a year of performing that song before I finally confided in Keri how uncomfortable I felt when I sang the song. I realized Santa Claus wasn't real, but Keri helped me connect the dots that Santa Claus in the song was actually the dad. It was a relief to learn that I wasn't singing about a mom having an affair with another man dressed up as Santa Claus.

A few years later, TKO had a performance scheduled in Richardson, Texas. I had a new song in my repertoire titled "Oh Happy Day" from the movie, Sister Act 2. Singing this song thrilled me. Sister Act 2 had become a favorite movie, playing on repeat at my house. While practicing, "Oh Happy Day," I sometimes nailed the high note at the end, but on other occasions, I fell short. Or, to be completely honest, at times I was way off, singing it a note or two below or above the pitch. It was frustrating because I knew I could nail the note, but on this particular day, I felt discouraged. Right before going out on stage, I confided in Marlene backstage, saying, "I don't think I can do it. I know I can't hit that high note today." Marlene knelt down to my level and reassured me, "Camey, sing and try because people will be proud of you. I believe in you; go out there and sing it like you mean it."

Taking a deep breath, I started singing. A crowd began to gather, stopping as they walked by. As I continued singing the song, the crowd grew even bigger. When the time came for the big note, I hit it in my falsetto voice, but the entire long note was off, and I knew that I had just blown it. Despite wanting to run off the stage, I kept going. When the song concluded, I walked off, attempting to control myself. However, I couldn't hold back my emotions any longer, and tears began to flow. I cried because of the disappointment I felt in myself for missing the note and feeling like a failure to Marlene and the group, who had given me the opportunity to sing this song.

Marlene, along with some other kids, came around the corner, picked me up, and cheered me on, emphasizing what an awesome job I did. They expressed excitement about performing with me at the next show.

As I packed up the TKO gig bag, a tall, handsome man and his daughter approached my mom and me. "Hey, what's your name?" he asked.

"Hi my name is Camey."

He shook my hand, "I'm Joe, and this is my daughter Ashlee. I just had to meet you and tell you that you did such a phenomenal job. I was blown away. I am so disappointed that my other daughter Jessica is not here; she would have loved to meet you. She too loves to sing and has a big voice like yours. Hopefully, we can catch your next show."

> "They weren't put off by my scars but interested in the story behind those scars."

During my time with TKO, I learned many kids have good hearts and I could trust them. They were rooting for me, not against me. They weren't put off by my scars but interested in the story behind those scars. I discovered that not only did kids want to get to know me, they too were proud of me. TKO taught me to know my worth without having to have someone clap for me. It was a realization that united us all in our shared pursuit of self-expression and excellence. Not just for fame but to share the gifts we knew God had given us.

TKO became my launching pad for public speaking and walking in God's confidence. Every moment in our lives has a purpose, as each experience adds new skills to our repertoire that we can draw upon in the future. I now have confidence that doesn't come from myself but from knowing that I am standing on Christ's firm foundation, the solid rock. In this season, I was equipped and trained to start the journey of telling my story.

CHAPTER TEN

My Extreme Makeover

For the past thirteen years, I had grown weary from undergoing more than fifteen surgeries. But it was time for a surgery I was looking forward to. I was genuinely excited at the potential opportunity to drastically alter my facial appearance. I was tired of the stares and questions, and I was now given the "green light" by my doctors for the biggest surgery of my life. This particular procedure held the weight of a lifetime of dreams—a moment of anticipation, a massive chapter I eagerly awaited. A week before the procedure, Dr. Hobar had me come in for a series of photos. It always felt real when I had to take pictures from various angles—what I call the "before" shots. I always dreaded looking at my "before" photos since my appearance never matched what I saw in my mind.

Dr. Hobar digitally altered the photos using new technology to give me a glimpse of what my nose and jaw would look like post-procedure, building my anticipation even more. He presented me with my new enhanced profile, which had been created by looking at some of my biological family's pictures to get the most accurate depiction of what my profile would have looked like if I had not been born with a cleft lip. Dr. Hobar detailed his plan to advance my maxilla (upper jaw) forward while simultaneously rotating my lower jaw (or mandible) backward by breaking my jaw to effectively address the most severe class 3 underbite. The jaw portion of the surgery, which focused on the alignment of my teeth by using braces, was to be a collaborative effort with Dr. Anderson-Cermin.

    Following this, Dr. Hobar used pieces of coral reef to enhance my cheekbones, which again was a groundbreaking technique. Simultaneously, Dr. Byrd, a pediatric plastic surgeon who worked alongside Dr. Hobar, would oversee my nose reconstruction operation, performing a detailed rhinoplasty surgery. Although a little bold, I took the opportunity to request a slight adjustment of my nose, asking Dr. Hobar to reduce the bump on my nose a bit more. There was a brief moment of hesitation, and then, with a warm smile, he nodded in agreement. It was amazing that my doctors allowed me, their patient, to work hand in hand with them as a team, and they "valued my voice." We collaborated like a championship team striving for victory, and I knew I was the one walking away with the trophy.

    Surgeries aren't without the possibility of complications. It was made clear to me from the start that they might need to cut my soft palate due to the significant movement of my mouth. We consulted a professional vocal coach, who directed us to seek a second opinion from a special doctor in Dallas, who was Barbra Streisand's former vocal doctor. The doctor stated that the cutting of my soft palate would undoubtedly impact my singing voice. Therefore, he strongly advised against the surgery at all costs. Despite this warning, at the age of thirteen, I was determined to undergo the surgery, even if it meant risking the potential loss of a voice that currently defined my identity. My doctors acknowledged the significance of my voice, and they assured me that they would do everything possible to avoid such an outcome, although the risk was present. My family, the doctors, and I fervently prayed for the best outcome—that my doctors wouldn't need to cut my soft palate and I would retain my voice.

Walking away from my visit with Dr. Hobar, I couldn't contain myself. I eagerly went to school bursting with enthusiasm and shared the news with all my friends about what I thought I would look like. Their responses weren't what I hoped for, as they were rather nonchalant, with a simple "That's cool," and then they would move right along. I wanted to believe they either couldn't fully grasp the extent of what was to come, or perhaps they thought I was exaggerating, as I tended to do at times. Their attitude was a reminder that this was my story, not theirs. I was aware that this surgery would be a significant, life-changing moment that could help heal the emotional scars of ridicule, social anxiety, and help me feel "normal." This excitement burned deep within me; yet, even I didn't fully grasp the extent of its impact.

Everyone told me this surgery was going to be a major one, but the thoughts of having my grand entrance to show the world my new look had clouded the reality about the upcoming pain and discomfort. However, it all became real the day before when I had to undergo pre-op blood work. I was absolutely terrified, fearing I might literally die from fear during the blood draw. In the past, I used to run around the room, trying to avoid nurses and doctors (remember my horrifying experience from the uncaring doctor), and it would take at least two or three staff to carry me back. But this time, I knew I had to toughen up; I was now thirteen years old, and I didn't want to appear too childish. I needed to mature a bit, but internally, I was just as nervous as I was at a young age.

After I entered the first room, they began by checking my vitals. I didn't enjoy the sensation of the blood pressure cuff, as it felt like it might squeeze a little too tightly and cut off my arm. However, I had undergone this process so many times that by now, I knew I wouldn't lose a limb from having my vitals checked. They weighed me at a whopping ninety pounds and just under five feet. Then I was told to go to room number two for the moment I had feared, the moment that had haunted my nightmares—the blood draw. The nurse had me sit down and extend my arm onto a cold table. She then tied a tourniquet tightly around my arm and swiped it with an alcohol swab. The moment was upon me when they would insert the needle. Mom asked if I wanted to hold her hand. I told her no, but secretly, I wanted to scream, "Yes, yes I do." I simply turned my face, closed my eyes tight, and held my breath as my mom calmly talked me through it. And then, there it was—the intense pinching sensation of the needle entering my arm. Mom reassured me that it was over, and once the needle was removed, I thought, "Wow, that wasn't as bad as I'd originally feared."

Now that the blood draw was behind me, my next source of anxiety revolved around two things. First, I knew I had to be NPO (from the Latin nil per os, nothing by mouth) by midnight, and second, perhaps the procedure I feared the most, was the IV insertion prior to surgery. I wasn't even concentrating on the post-recovery pain, as I thought I could handle that. The idea of needing to be NPO by midnight was quite dreadful. If I hadn't been told that, it wouldn't have been such a big deal, but just the thought of not being able to eat or drink made me want to eat or drink more before the clock struck midnight. I was so nervous that I stayed up all night processing everything that might happen. It was as though I saw the previews of the movie before the movie would begin. I went to bed thinking about how thirsty I was, ruminating about the impending IV procedure in the morning. It was a lot for my thirteen-year-old brain to comprehend fully. I knew that it was very important to not eat or drink because I'd been told during one of my previous surgeries that I had aspirated. The anesthesiologist was furious with my mom, falsely accusing her, stating that she could have killed me by allowing me to eat—which she did not! But still, the fear of death lingered in my mind. One more mental scar created by someone in a profession that was supposed to heal not hurt.

Fortunately, during this time, several things brought me immense comfort: my doctors, whom I trusted with my life, quite literally; my blanket; and last but not least, my family. I was also extremely excited about my upcoming extreme makeover. On my way to the hospital at 4:30 a.m., my body was tired, but my mind was wide awake. To prepare for surgery, I had to put on a gown (which, since I was a kid, they allowed me to keep my underwear on, a relief for my modest and embarrassed self). I always eagerly anticipated the "silly juice," as they called it, also known as Versed, which I knew would start working in about twenty to thirty minutes, and it allowed me to have a little sip of fluid as well. Then, the anesthesiologist would come in and discuss my options for the IV insertion. "Camey, we can apply a topical numbing agent, which won't numb your skin entirely, or I can insert the IV once you're asleep." Most kids choose to fall asleep first, but in my case, that meant having the nitrous oxide mask applied, which was a firm no, as this triggered extreme anxiety in me.

    I successfully endured the IV insertion with topical numbing cream, and with pride, not a single tear escaped my eyes this round. Next, I recall Dr. Hobar instructing the anesthesiologist to administer a calming medication via my IV. Despite my efforts to maintain composure, Dr. Hobar, sensing my nervousness, insisted on the additional dose which I needed. I can still picture the nurses wheeling me out of pre-op, where I exchanged hugs with my dad and mom. Though I was determined not to reveal my anxiety through tears, the emotions welled up, and I felt the pressure building in my throat and behind my eyes. I wanted to project maturity, but at that moment, the "silly juice" hit me like a freight train, and I was gone. Nothing else mattered from that point forward. I have a vague recollection of the nurse pressing the elevator button, but everything beyond that moment remains an anesthesia-induced haze.

    My parents informed me that during the course of my surgery Dr. Hobar, Dr. Cermin-Anderson, and Dr. Byrd took several opportunities to visit with them in the waiting room and keep them updated on my progress. Dr. Hobar reassured them, saying, "The surgery is going exceptionally well. Dr. Byrd is currently working on her nose. I will join him shortly. Everything is progressing as planned. I want to make additional adjustments since we're already addressing specific areas, so she won't have to return later for another surgery. Afterward, she'll be swollen, with bruising, and her jaws will be wired shut—almost unrecognizable. It's a big procedure, but she's a fighter, and with such supportive parents, I'm confident she'll navigate the recovery process successfully." With my parents' agreement, he, along with Dr. Anderson-Cermin, Dr. Byrd, and the entire surgical staff, dedicated thirteen hours to working on me that day.

THE ENCOUNTER

I found myself seated on the softest, most vibrant green grass under the gaze of an intensely bright blue sky surrounded by rolling hills. Sitting under a tree, I engaged in conversation with a man. I noticed His brown hair, but it was His mesmerizing brown eyes that pierced my heart, and an overwhelming peace covered me. While all the details of our discussion have faded from memory, the awareness of our precious time together still remains. As our dialogue neared its end, He reassured me that the challenges ahead would be tough, but I possessed strength and bravery. My expression of uncertainty about the arduous journey that lay ahead was met by His fixed gaze as He looked into my eyes and told me that He would be with me always and never leave me. At that precise moment, a faint yet resonant call seemed to roll over the distant hills, interrupting our exchange: "Camey ... Camey, your surgery is over." In an instant, I found myself whisked away, surrounded by a luminous expanse of bright white light.

Amid the gentle hum of beeping machines, I strained to perceive my surroundings. Through the haze of ointment coating my eyes, a comforting voice reached me—Dr. Hobar expressed, "I am so proud of you. You did great, Camey." My vision, although still blurry, allowed me to discern the walls behind him adorned with my before-and-computer-altered photos, each meticulously marked with measurements. Despite the persistent yearning to return to the comforting embrace of my dream, the tangible reality of the completed surgery asserted itself with undeniable clarity.

Since my arms were not restrained, I attempted to remove the mask over my nose but was halted by a nurse who grabbed my arm, mindful of the numerous sutures on my lip. The anesthesiologist, sensing discomfort, adjusted the mask from the top of my mouth and nose, lowering the mask to allow blow-by oxygen. My throat felt sore from the endotracheal tube, and as I was wheeled into the recovery room, nurses repeatedly said, "Camey, take a deep breath. Your surgery is over." While being wheeled to the recovery room in the ICU, I had my eyes closed and I couldn't manage to speak, but I was able to ask my mom a question in sign language. I touched my throat and then mimicked scissors with my hand. In response, she reassured me, "No, they did not have to cut your soft palate." Relief crossed my face, and with a contented sigh, I drifted back to sleep.

MY REFLECTION

In the subsequent days, I found myself confined to the ICU, and later, I transitioned to a step-down floor. While memories of the ICU are a blur, fragments of my time in the step-down unit remain etched in my mind. A piece of advice reached my mom's ears—a suggestion that it might not be wise for me to confront my altered reflection just yet, as I was extremely swollen, black and blue, and with hundreds of stitches on my lip. Yet, an undeniable eagerness within me yearned to catch a glimpse of the enhanced version of Camey. Despite the internal conflict and a lingering doubt about the reality matching my expectations, an inner voice urged me to satisfy my curiosity.

Balancing on the edge of anticipation and apprehension, I reached an agreement with myself to face the truth. Armed with a soup spoon (that I could not use), I aimed for the best view from the spoon's reflection, only to be met with a sight that felt far from pleasant. What lay before me resembled a massive nose adorned with intricate stitches, reminiscent of spider legs, extending across my upper lip.

Every time my liquid meals arrived, my spoon continued its exploration of different areas of my face, a futile attempt to comprehend the changes. Recognizing the unproductiveness, I appealed to my mom to allow me to rinse my mouth at the sink with a mirror. After a moment of contemplation, she consented. Weak from the surgery, with her support, I made my way to the sink very slowly. It was my first time out of bed, and I held my Foley catheter taped to my leg. As spit dribbled from the side of my numb mouth, I lifted my head to face my reflection.

What I saw was a small-framed girl in a hospital gown, her hair in disarray, perhaps a consequence of the gel used in the operating room, and pulled into a high ponytail. Bruising adorned my eyes, my lips were swollen, and an intricate network of stitches peppered my upper lip—hundreds of them. While the reflection before me seemed an improvement from the spoon's version, it still fell short of my envisioned image. Yet, as my eyes traversed from right to left, a profound realization struck—the reflection didn't quite resemble Camey. Who was this person?

The sharpness of my jawline and the visible tip of my nose caught my attention, yet the arch and outer nostrils remained concealed beneath a solid white bandage. At that moment, a glimmer of hope emerged. The girl staring back at me possessed gentle and caring eyes, and I sensed the essence of a good person.

While I was in my hospital room, all my siblings visited, which brought me such a sense of home and overwhelming love. A nephew and niece came to say hello, but they didn't recognize me initially and were scared, but I did not hold that against them. I later learned that Mom gave each sibling a pep talk before seeing me, ensuring that they were prepared for what they were about to encounter and to minimize any surprised or scared expressions. I wasn't able to speak. My jaws were wired shut for eight weeks, which presented a major challenge. Consequently, my primary mode of communication was through writing.

Despite the challenges, I had some lighthearted moments, one being when my sister, Piper, wrote me a response to something I'd written her, only to suddenly realize and laugh, "Hey, why am

I writing you back? I can talk to you!" It was a humorous reminder of the situation.

It didn't take me long to adapt to this writing-based form of communication. Of course, my preferred mode of communication was speech, but soon I developed some ventriloquist skills, making the best of a challenging situation. Again, my family could understand me for the most part, but others couldn't, which left me frustrated and resulted in me having to write for better communication.

Mom reminded me that my best friend, Jessica, brought me a card signed by the entire eighth grade class, along with a stuffed bear. Even though I couldn't fully recall this memory, the memory of the kindness from Jessica, her parents, and my classmates brought me the encouragement I needed to heal.

JUST KEEP WALKING

As I learned to navigate the hospital unit floor, each step became a symbol of triumph over the possibility of blood clots. The collective strength of my family's cheers reverberated like a melody of encouragement. This became the cadence that propelled me forward. Their consistent affirmations instilled a sense of unity, making me feel I wasn't confronting this challenge in isolation. Shelly, my oldest sister, much like a second mom, was a supportive presence that infused my weakening limbs with determination, having me hold onto my IV pole while she assisted me with the support of my other arm.

During our stroll around the unit, Shelly openly shared her empathy for the hardships I was enduring. "Camey, I'm genuinely sorry that you have to go through all this; it's a lot for anyone to bear."

Pausing, I turned to her, gazed deeply into her eyes, and said with my best ventriloquist skills, so she would understand, "Oh, but my condition can be fixed; there are others in this hospital who may not find a cure, as their healing awaits them on the other side of Heaven."

A moment of quiet reflection ensued as Shelly absorbed my words. "That's deep."

Later, she contemplated how this perspective truly shifted her understanding of the challenges faced by others.

MIDNIGHT CALL

In the wake of my post-surgery recovery, I wanted the reassuring presence of my mom, my comforter and protector, at all times throughout my entire hospital stay. However, one night, anxiety crept in, manifesting as a struggle to draw a full breath. Stirring in the silence of the night, I made two unsettling discoveries. First, my mom was absent, which sparked initial panic. Later I realized that she likely needed a break; something that, as a mom, I now fully understand. Second, I observed blood flowing back up my IV tubing, and a chilling fear seized me; I was convinced I was on the brink of bleeding to death. These two discoveries triggered a full-blown panic attack.

Summoning the nurse through the call bell in the dead of night proved futile. Multiple attempts yielded no response. After what felt like an eternity, a nurse finally arrived. Her demeanor lacked empathy as she curtly warned me to calm down or face the prospect of waking Dr. Hobar. At that moment, I didn't feel like I was asking too much. I pleaded silently, not wanting to inconvenience my doctor. My requests for assistance went unheeded, with the nurse opting to notify Dr. Hobar instead of addressing my immediate concerns about the IV tubing.

Around 2:00 a.m., a knock echoed through the doors, and I wasn't sure if it was the nurse, my mom, or my doctor, but there stood Dr. Hobar. His entrance mirrored that of a comforting father figure, radiating a calming presence. With assurance in his voice, he comforted me, promising that everything would be okay. He told me he could give me something to help calm me down, but I found solace in his mere presence. In that moment, he knew too that I was going to be all right, and a profound sense of peace washed over me. All was well, and he was able to have the nurse change out my IV fluids, which was causing the blood to back up into the IV line due to pressure difference. I was finally able to get rest. Dr. Hobar's continued concern and unending care truly granted me the ability to feel safe. His desire to help others was able to outweigh all my negative experiences with other medical professionals.

MUSICAL NOTE

The following day brought an unexpected visitor, her gentle presence announced by a tender knock on the door. In walked a woman of breathtaking beauty, her eyes radiant with a poised expression of love and grace. Her voice, a soothing melody, resonated with kindness as she bestowed upon me a thoughtful, heartfelt gift. To my surprise, it was none other than Mrs. Hobar, Dr. Hobar's wife. She presented me with a silver musical note charm bracelet, a gesture that left me in awe. The fact that Dr. Hobar's wife had come to visit, let alone bring such a special gift, was a healing balm, especially considering the disruption I unintentionally caused to their family the night before. Beyond the material beauty of the bracelet, it was her profound thoughtfulness that touched me deeply. In that moment, I felt more than just loved. Former Prime Minister Harold Macmillan once said, "No man succeeds without a good woman behind him. Wife or mother, if it is both, he is twice blessed indeed." The essence of his words resonated, and I felt doubly blessed by her presence.

Dr. Hobar's surgical plan successfully allowed me to live the life God had intended for me. He meticulously repaired my face to look like what it should have looked like without the cleft lip. He has demonstrated himself to be not only an expert craftsman and artist but also an expert in the science and techniques of his field. I will never have the words to adequately express my gratitude to him for changing my life.

NASAL TRUMPET

In the midst of my recovery, I encountered a new anxiety. The wiring of my jaws and the aftermath of nose and mouth reconstruction caused obstructions primarily due to dried blood so I was forced to breathe through my mouth. This triggered panic attacks and labored breathing. Routine checks of my oxygen saturation levels by the medical staff consistently showed a range of 92–95 percent, indicating that my oxygen levels were ranging between low-normal and normal. Yet, the sensation that I wasn't receiving enough oxygen persisted. A pivotal moment occurred when Dr. Hobar entered my room and acknowledged the need to address my breathing discomfort. He knew what needed to be done to alleviate my anxiety and help restore my breathing. He delegated the task, unable to perform it himself because of his enduring love toward me, knowing the pain and discomfort it would cause. The compassionate new, may I add handsome, young intern explained the procedure and presented what resembled a water hose tube with a trumpet-like end—called a nasal trumpet. He intended to insert it into my nose, extending it to the back of my throat, facilitating easier breathing. When I inquired about potential pain, he honestly stated that he had never had nasal trumpets inserted but reassured me it probably would not hurt but could be uncomfortably invasive. He advised me to swallow as he initiated the insertion.

    The intern coated the nasal trumpet with lubrication and then squeezed its edges to fit into my nostril. He then began a twisting motion to navigate the tube through my right nostril. The initial twist proved surprisingly painless, but subsequent rotations were far from pleasant. Each turn seemed to dislodge dried blood and stitches, momentarily impeding my breathing. I struggled with the need to breathe and swallow while accommodating the tube's passage through my nasal passages. Fearing suffocation, I opened my lips as wide and far back as possible, allowing air to flow through the open space between my teeth and cheeks to facilitate better airflow. Once the procedure concluded, the aftermath felt odd and uncomfortable, especially when I swallowed. I felt the tube in the back of my throat, reminiscent of the lingering sensation of having an endotracheal tube.

As he prepared to address the second nasal passage, the intern detected my apprehension. Reluctantly, I braced myself for the inevitable. As the second nasal trumpet was inserted, tears welled up in my eyes and a few escaped. Along with a tinge of embarrassment, considering the intern's youth and attractiveness, the entire experience was one more in a line of traumatic events that added layers to my scars.

But almost immediately, I noticed a significant improvement in my breathing, as if a weight had been lifted. The nasal trumpets remained in place for about a week, and the procedure to remove them seemed relatively straightforward. But unbeknownst to me (and the doctors), the removal of one nasal trumpet would impact not only my future breathing but also the future appearance of my nose. Today, I carry a subtle aesthetic asymmetry, with one nostril slightly larger than the other, a lasting reminder of that pivotal moment in my recovery.

BACK TO SCHOOL

Alongside my wired jaws, I had a silicone bandage on my upper lip, a protective shield against the looming threat of keloid scarring. In an attempt to resume normalcy and out of excitement to show off my new look, I returned to school despite my parents' hesitation. Returning post-surgery would come with physical and mental struggles. Although my parents repeatedly assured me of my intelligence, my grades seemed to tell a different narrative, suggesting I was at the bottom of my class. The delicate dance between surgery and schooling persisted as a significant challenge, leaving me a bit further behind with each medical intervention. Nevertheless, my friends were the driving force for my return, not necessarily my studies.

Lunchtime, typically a routine affair, became a unique challenge as I navigated the necessity of eating from a syringe. I would insert the plastic tube into the side of my mouth where my back teeth meet. This allowed me to eat through the tube connected to a syringe with liquefied foods since my mouth was still wired completely shut. I had lost some sensation on the sides of my chin, so at times food would find its way oozing down my chin without my awareness. Yet, my friends remained defenders of unwavering support, graciously looking in the opposite direction and overlooking the quirks and challenges of my altered eating habits and my attempts at ventriloquist speech through clenched teeth.

After about a week of reintegration, I acknowledged the toll it was taking on my still-recovering body. Recognizing the need for a respite, I made the decision to take a couple more weeks off from school. Looking back, it was the best choice given the delicate state of my recovery.

Observing the reactions of my peers and my responses to them still intrigues me. While internally, I knew I was the same Camey, the external transformation was undeniable. Adjusting to my new look required time for my friends to peer beyond the altered appearance and rediscover the "real me" beneath the changed exterior. The path back to a sense of normalcy was a delicate dance of understanding and acceptance, both on my part and from those around me.

As days moved on, at only eighty-four pounds, the focal point of my recovery shifted toward the arduous task of regaining lost weight. And another surgery was looming, scheduled within the next few months, a delicate procedure involving the attachment of a vein from my lower lip to my upper lip. While promising improved blood flow, this surgical endeavor would once again render me incapable of separating my lips for approximately two weeks, binding them in the middle together by a delicate thread or more accurately, a vital vein.

In this chapter of my recovery, sustenance consisted solely of liquids and pureed foods, a culinary landscape where milkshakes and mashed potatoes took center stage. I evolved into a connoisseur of pureed concoctions, crafting my own peculiar yet strangely satisfying combinations—mashed potatoes topped with ranch dressing or Kraft Mac and Cheese transformed into a velvety puree.

There is a poignant memory etched into my consciousness—a moment of frustration and despair. I struggled to push pureed food through a syringe, and its rubber attachment was strained by the effort. In this instance, attempting to force down a piece of ground beef without chewing seemed prohibited, yet where there was a will, there was a way. I was so tired of liquid food. My mom, sensing my frustration, assured me everything would be okay and that this, too, shall pass. My response was bitter, tinged with sadness and anger, which betrayed my exhaustion. In that trying moment, she offered steady reassurance, acknowledging the immense difficulty of my journey and emphasizing that it would be all right. The specifics of how I navigated through that particular day remain somewhat unclear. But the memory of utter exhaustive frustration is strong. With the support and love of my family, I continued to take small steps each day, which provided me with the strength to persevere and overcome.

THE WIRE

The anticipation of the momentous occasion—removing the wires that bound my jaws shut—was tainted with an unexpected revelation. An ominous pain nestled in the recesses of my upper jaws that I could only feel once the wires on my mouth were removed. It was an unfamiliar sensation, akin to a persistent jab in the back cheek whenever I attempted to part my jaws. The discomfort escalated with each futile effort, discouraging me from opening my mouth wider than necessary.

Accustomed to occasional discomfort from years of wearing braces, I summoned the courage to address this peculiar pain. A visit to Dr. Cermin-Anderson was necessary, and as she delicately wiped a small dental mirror against my cheek to defog it, even the gentlest pull of my cheek flesh elicited a wince. Dr. Cermin-Anderson, with genuine concern etched on her face, exclaimed, "Oh, gosh, Camey, how long has this been hurting you?" My response was, "It's been for the past week since my wires were cut, but I've especially noticed it whenever I open my mouth." Silence hung in the air as Dr. Cermin-Anderson contemplated my words.

A somber realization descended as Dr. Cermin-Anderson turned to her beloved assistant, Nora, and they exchanged glances that conveyed a shared concern. Then, turning to my mom and me, Dr. Cermin-Anderson uttered, "I'm so sorry, but these two wires on your upper jaw were accidentally left in your mouth after surgery. They were supposed to come out shortly after surgery." Weeks passed, and some of my mouth tissue had grown over the wire that was attached to my bone.

Dr. Cermin-Anderson endeavored to rectify the situation by attempting to untwist the wire lodged in the back of my mouth. Each twist, however, caused me to involuntarily clench the arms of the dental chair as tears escaped down my face. I was trying to appear stoic and composed, but at only thirteen years old, I was unable to suppress the surge of emotions. I was a mess.

With tears mirrored in Dr. Cermin-Anderson's eyes, she conceded, "Camey, I can't." She relinquished the hemostats. Her assistant echoed the sentiment: "I'm sorry, Camey, I can't do this either." A brief silence ensued before a new figure entered the scene—an assertive, young male dentist with noticeably strong arms. His determined demeanor suggested a commitment to resolve the issue with the utmost kindness, emblematic of Children's Hospital Dallas's approach.

Presented with options, I braced myself for the discomfort that lay ahead. The dentist proposed a swift extraction without anesthesia or multiple numbing injections, the latter being a prospect as unpalatable as the former. Opting for the former without numbing injections, I consented to the procedure, ready to endure the pain and challenges it held.

With hemostats in hand, the dentist embarked on the intricate task. Each twist, accompanied by the sound of tearing tissue and dried blood, evoked an internal struggle. Despite the evident pain, I remained silent as tears traced their way down my cheeks. On the third pull, my head lifted off the dental chair, but the wire remained intact. He then exerted more force, holding my head down with his other hand, prompting a sensation akin to a zipper being unzipped, tissue and dried blood tearing apart as the wire was finally removed.

He sought my approval to proceed to the other side, delicately suggesting the possibility of anesthesia but anesthesia was a notion I vehemently rejected. Thus, I bravely opted for him to tackle the other side. This time, with the dentist's use of heightened force and a firm grip on my shoulders, the ordeal concluded with a single, decisive pull. In the aftermath, tears filled the eyes of my mom, Dr. Cermin-Anderson, Nora, and even the steadfast dentist.

CATCHING UP

After months of wearing the silicone bandage on my upper lip, I finally received the green light to remove it. I could finally apply my CoverGirl powdered makeup, which helped smooth out some of the harsh lines, though softer than before, on my lip. The physical scars were healing, but the mental and emotional toll of each surgery still left me feeling inadequate and academically inferior. I was back at school by then, and everyone else seemed to know things I knew nothing about, and I struggled to catch up. I was overwhelmed, and I often came home in tears, feeling stupid.

My parents constantly reassured me that I wasn't stupid and that I just needed time to catch up. But, much like most teenagers, I felt like they didn't fully understand what I was going through. I pleaded with them to let me drop certain subjects, and eventually, they agreed and allowed me to only take elective subjects like art and music for the remainder of my eighth grade year, completing the core subjects at home so I could catch up. This decision relieved me from the added pressure of failing grades and allowed me to socialize more with my friends. At this time some of the guys who had been my friends prior to the surgery were now giving me encouraging glances and engaging in more conversations with me. I enjoyed this newfound attention and the boost to my self-esteem.

CHAPTER ELEVEN
No Mountains in This Valley

My "extreme makeover" marked a significant divide in my life's timeline—the period before this pivotal surgery and after it. It took some time for me to walk past the mirror and realize that the person looking back was truly me. I felt proud of the person I saw, acknowledging the hard work of my doctors, family, and even myself. Despite the outward physical changes, I remained the same person inside.

The experience also brought to light the harsh reality of acceptance versus rejection based on appearance, not just for me but also among my friends. I was surprised by how some friends distanced themselves as the result of my changed appearance. This became a defining moment with my classmates, revealing who my true friends were, those who cared about me regardless of my looks. It was devastating to hear that some had considered me disgusting to look at pre-surgery, as they were now telling me to my face, as though it was funny. Did they not realize they were talking to the same girl? Apparently not.

Just as I was starting to feel comfortable with my new looks and adjusting to changed friendships, my parents dropped what felt like an atomic bomb. I was blindsided by the news: they felt called to move to the Rio Grande Valley on the Texas-Mexican border to learn Spanish, intending to become missionaries to the interior of Mexico.

When my parents shared details about this part of Texas, called the Valley, my mind painted a picture of an oasis of mountains, meandering rivers, lush palm trees, and the gorgeous South Padre Island beach on the Gulf Coast. Furthermore, my mom captivated my interest by mentioning that my prospective school, Valley Christian School (VCS), had a cheerleading team—an enticing prospect that wasn't available at my current school, Grace Preparatory Academy (GPA). Since childhood, I'd harbored dreams of being a cheerleader, complete with twirly skirts, pom-poms, and the possibility of gaining some attention from boys.

However, getting me into the car destined for the Valley proved to be a challenging task. I stalled and, when I thought about getting in the car, froze in my tracks. I was not physically able to make myself move. My resistance was so grave that Mom resorted to calling Dad, who was staying behind for a couple of weeks to complete a roofing job that would sustain our family financially for the rest of the year. He demanded that I get in the car, which I finally did. It was known in my family that you did not refuse Dad—not because of what might happen, but because you never wanted to disappoint him.

God's protective hand seemed to be over Mom and me as we drove more than eight hours to the Valley, as we encountered a couple of setbacks along the way. The clouds above us had an unusual appearance, something I'd never seen before. Mom pulled off to a small, oddly placed gas station in no-man's land. It was a sturdy structure with only two gas pumps, entirely made of concrete. While Mom was inside paying for gas and I was grabbing a snack, a gust of wind shook the building, causing cans to fall off the shelves. Peering through the glass windows, we witnessed a funnel cloud passing over us. To make matters worse, a large white cloud, resembling a rain cloud, approached and dropped large hailstones. Fortunately, our car received no evidence of hail damage, and in the midst of a tornado and hailstorm, we drove nine hours through the chaos, and miraculously arrived unscathed in the middle of the night at King's Way language school in McAllen, Texas.

Slowly, I made my way up three steps in the darkness and into the white wooden duplex, which resembled a trailer home elevated on cement blocks. I couldn't help but turn my gaze to what appeared to be black metal bars covering the windows. As I stepped onto the rickety wooden floors, a distinct scent of mustiness filled the air, emanating from the aging wood. Despite its flaws, we settled down for the night, exhausted from our long drive. Thankfully, my dad had already brought our belongings in a moving van a few weeks prior.

When morning arrived, the view from my tiny room window utterly shattered my expectations. Instead of a valley lined by beautiful mountains, all I saw was what resembled a barren desert, sprinkled with palm trees, stretching as far as my eyes could see, with a lone tumbleweed literally blowing in the breeze. It was like something from an old Western movie. The promised mountains were nowhere in sight.

The next morning marked my introduction to VCS in Mission, Texas. As we drove there, we passed multiple colonias—makeshift communities with trailers and lean-tos that lacked adequate water, plumbing, and sometimes even electricity. I had never seen such poverty in my life. At my new school, a three-day meet and greet before school officially started was underway, and the reality of my unfamiliar surroundings hit me hard. I was now a part of the majority because of the color of my skin; however, I felt like a minority because I did not identify with this culture. At my previous school, I was the only girl with a "tan" complexion. Now I found myself in one of the lowest socioeconomic areas in the United States, surrounded by unfamiliar faces with diverse accents and speaking a language I didn't understand. I experienced culture shock, to say the least! As I tried to navigate this new environment, I not only felt like an outsider but I was an outsider, and I yearned for this nightmare to soon be over. I prayed to wake up back at my old school and in my old home. To make matters worse, the school was in chaos as they were short-handed; thus, Mom was roped into helping. The overwhelming sense of displacement weighed heavily on me as I wrestled internally with the stark lifestyle differences and the surreal feeling of being in an unfamiliar place. I thought to myself, "I'm not in the US anymore, yet I know I'm not in Mexico...where am I?"

On the last day of the school meet and greet, as my mom and I were preparing to go home, we walked through the gym and unexpectedly ran into the elementary school principal, Nancy Armstrong. Mom, much like Dad, never met a stranger and struck up a friendly conversation about the school and engaged in small talk. I, on the other hand, was simply not in the mood, feeling done with the whole school experience. I wasn't rude, but I also wasn't my usual engaging self.

Nancy shared that her family had recently moved from Arkansas, and her husband was a music minister at a Baptist church in Edinburg, a city nearby. She inquired about my grade, and her face lit up as she mentioned having a son in my class. My attention waned, as I didn't remember meeting her son at the meet and greet, but my attention returned abruptly as a tall guy entered the gym through a side door, wrapping electrical cords in his hand. Nancy turned around and introduced him, saying, "Oh, Judi and Camey, speaking of my son, this is Nathan."

As Nathan approached, I could tell he was shy, but he extended a friendly handshake to my mom before greeting me with a handshake of his own. When our eyes met, I was captivated by the striking brilliance of the blue color in his gaze. We exchanged pleasantries, and while it didn't seem significant at the time, it was a relief to discover that another classmate was "white" and could speak English because, until that moment, I felt like an outsider.

THE NEW GIRL

I was going to be the new girl in school, and no one there knew about all the challenges I'd faced—my surgeries, my struggles with school, and my grades. And I decided they didn't need to know. After all, I'd undergone my "extreme makeover" and gained newfound confidence, so this could be a fresh start.

As I set foot in VCS on that first day, all my positive confidence dissipated. I discovered we were assigned a locker, a novelty for me since they didn't exist in my previous school. However, learning to decipher the locker code became a challenge for me, and those familiar feelings of stupidity began to rise.

By divine intervention, my locker happened to be right under Nathan's, and I was grateful we had met previously in the gym. I asked him for help, and he generously shared the trick—turn right first, then left, and circle back around. Nathan effortlessly opened my locker on his first try, and it appeared the mystery was solved. However, subsequent days saw me still struggling with our old red school lockers. I hesitated to ask Nathan repeatedly, feeling that I might be wearing out my welcome. To combat this, I adjusted the code to make it easier for me or left it unlocked altogether, knowing I didn't have any valuables inside.

Nathan and I found ourselves assigned to seats in close proximity in the majority of our classes. I was drawn to his Arkansas accent. It carried with it a sense of familiarity and safety reminiscent of the comforting presence of friends back in Dallas.

Trying to make conversation, I couldn't resist inquiring about the specific part of Arkansas he was from. In his distinctive drawl, he replied, "My family moved from Camden." The mention of Camden sparked a distant recollection within me. Camden, I thought. Without much thought at all, I quickly grabbed my wallet, retrieving a photograph of a girl I had met while on a summer singing tour with a group called the Young Continental Singers.

In my innocence, I did not question the logic behind pulling out a seemingly random picture to make a connection with an entire state. It was as if I were attempting to find a needle in a haystack, an impulse that now would seem misguided but at the time seemed relevant. As I turned the picture over to show Nathan, expecting perhaps a casual acknowledgment, I was met with a look of confusion. He exclaimed, "I know this girl. This is LeAnn!" The sheer improbability of such a connection left us marveling at the intricate threads that seemed to weave our lives together in this new and unfamiliar place. What were the odds? This revelation helped ease my anxiety and continued to remind me that God is in the details, even when we don't want to get in the car.

HE NEVER FAILED ME

At VCS, most of the high school students spoke Spanish. In the early weeks, students began conversing with me in Spanish, and I'm certain I met their attempts with a perplexed expression because I had no idea what they were saying. This led to some teasing since there was an irony in my being Hispanic, yet not fluent in Spanish, and maybe some students thought I was intentionally avoiding the language.

Because of my past wounds, I hesitated to share my adoption story but resorted to explaining myself sooner than I would have preferred. I found myself having to share a condensed version whenever others pressed me in conversation. Typically, this disclosure would put an end to the inquiries, while others told me I should know Spanish because it's in my blood—whatever that meant! I encountered attempts from others who tried to teach me Spanish, which unbeknownst to me mostly focused on inappropriate words. All of this added to my confusion about who I really was, and what I was doing in this place.

Despite the negatives, the school had its positives that helped me stay afloat. I did make the cheerleading team and it became a source of joy, and I excelled at it. Making it on the varsity volleyball team added another accomplishment to my list of successes. I was also voted homecoming queen and my grades were excelling—I was now a straight-A student with little effort. The academic standards at this school were not as stringent as my previous school, which allowed me to move from a B student, with some Cs, and a few As sprinkled in for good measure, to finding my place on the honor roll and holding the third position in my class. Admittedly, being third out of twelve students might not sound groundbreaking, but it was a noteworthy achievement for me and was a great boost in my confidence.

It's important to note that VCS was connected to a children's home, bringing in a diverse student population. Forty percent of the students came from broken homes or no homes at all, while 30 percent were individuals who had faced the stigma of being labeled dropouts from other schools. The remaining 30 percent of students were from families in the area, children of faculty members, and even a few students who came across the border from Mexico every morning to attend an English-speaking school. VCS was a departure from the polished environment of my previous school in Dallas. However, one day I unexpectedly stumbled upon a classroom that took my breath away from the moment I stepped in. The high school music room welcomed me with walls painted in a soothing light blue decorated with spray-painted artwork of black and white piano keys, accompanied by captivating murals. In one corner stood an old upright piano, its panel off, exposing the delicate strings within.

After the music teacher entered, he skillfully played chords that resonated with my soul—chords reminiscent of those I had only heard Wilda play. When the kids in the music class began to sing, I was enchanted by the tight harmonies. My amazement reached new heights when a young girl, my age, descended toward the piano to lead a song, her voice full of emotion echoing the soulful resonance of Lauren Hill from Sister Act 2 that sent chills up and down my body.

It was a defining moment in my life when I thought to myself, "Okay, Camey, you can do this. Let down your guard and enjoy music again." No one at that school had heard me sing, but I slowly began to let my peers see the real me, my friendliness and outgoing nature. I added music as one of my electives. I learned that the music class had a side group called the Cornerstone Singers who would embark on a summer-long tour around the United States bringing in money for the children's home. I thought without hesitation, "I'm in!"

Nathan, or Nate to his friends, shared with me that his dad was a music minister at their church. Aware of my passion for music and having heard me lead a few songs in music class, Nate expressed his own love for singing. However, I had only heard him sing in class, and then only faintly as he sang with other boys. Nate's personality was both shy and humble, but mainly shy since he didn't initiate conversations or look people in the eye when he spoke. Curious, I asked him if he was going to audition for the summer singing trip. Initially, he said no, but to my amazement, on the day of auditions, as I was waiting for my turn, I suddenly heard this smooth, buttery, beautiful, full, soulful, and strong male tenor voice that I'd never heard before. Nate's older brother, Tim, and younger brother, Bryan, were waiting in the hallway, when I expressed my amazement at the voice I'd just heard, Tim responded with a smile, saying, "Yeah, he did it . . . he auditioned."

I met Nate as he walked out of the music room, still stunned by his voice, a voice that could put to shame any boy band vocals. I asked him quickly, "How did it go?" I knew it was my turn next. "I think it went well . . . we'll see," he responded with a shrug. Still intimidated by Nate's amazing voice, butterflies overwhelmed my stomach as I walked in. My vocal teacher started with scales first, and then asked me to sing the song that we'd been working on in class: "He Never Failed Me Yet."

Reading the teacher's facial expressions, I was sure I hadn't made the cut; he didn't seem overly enthused by my audition. I was disappointed and kept replaying all my mistakes in my mind as I waited for the results. After a long couple of days, the results were posted. Hesitantly, I looked and saw Nate's name, which I knew was a given. Going down the list alphabetically, I finally saw my last name—Thompson. We'd both made it and would be touring with the Cornerstone Singers!

SUMMER LOVE

That summer was fun as everyone in the group became undeniably close. Nate could have asked lots of other girls to sit with him on the tour bus, but he chose to sit next to me, much to the other girls' disappointment. We spent hours discussing everything from our feelings about moving to the Valley our freshman year and him embracing his new beginnings while I fought them, to our goals in life, our dreams, and our mutual love for the Lord. We explored music, discussing various genres, as he was well-versed in all of them. And I shared with Nate that my musical upbringing was primarily rooted in Christian music. While my parents didn't oppose other genres, I found comfort in what was familiar. I conveyed my appreciation for the soulful tunes of artists like Whitney Houston, Boyz II Men, and Brian McKnight. Brian McKnight happened to be Nate's all-time favorite vocalist, which was no surprise to me, as Nate's voice sounded much like his.

Nate then revealed his extensive CD collection, a treasure trove of hundreds of albums. It felt like having my own personal jukebox. He invited me to choose the next CD to listen to, given that he had so many. During our music exploration, he brought up the groups 4Him and Phillips, Craig, and Dean. I was surprised that he knew about them, and equally surprised that he knew all the "old"

Christian groups. It turned out that these groups had played a role earlier in his life, helping him learn harmony parts.

THE KISS

I wasn't sure what to expect during this summer-long tour with the Cornerstone Singers; however, having the opportunity to get to know everyone was a blast, and I'm so glad I was afforded the opportunity to take on this adventure. The summer was coming to a close and our concert for Cornerstone Singer's tour was in Houston at a small church. I had just shared my testimony, highlighting the significance of having three fathers: my dad, Rea; my biological father, Jesús; and, of course, my spiritual father, God. My parents were visiting friends in Houston, so I would return to the Valley with them. This was the end of my summer tour, and I knew I would be saying goodbye to friends that had become family and to my seat on the bus next to Nate. He had become my "special friend" as Mom referred to him. There was an undeniable spark between us, like a magnet pulling us closer and closer. I knew I wouldn't see Nate again until we started school in our tenth-grade year.

 I mentioned to Nate after the concert that I needed to grab my things off the bus. Without hesitation, he volunteered to help and without intention, we found ourselves alone on the bus while everyone was finishing in the church. We had a short conversation about the summer and all we had learned about each other and how thankful we were to have met. Then, I turned around in what felt like slow motion, leaned in toward him, and grabbed his necktie to pull his six-foot, three-inch self down toward me. While I was on my tiptoes, we shared a short, sweet kiss. I could feel the chills that left me with goosebumps, while Nate was not able to utter a word. Afraid we would be caught by someone looking for us, I was now in a hurry. Nate later told me that he knew at that moment with his first kiss that he had found his first love. I had no way of knowing it at the tender age of fourteen, but moving to South Texas and meeting Nate would change my life forever. Our relationship would have many highs and lows, but for now I would relish this new beautiful friendship.

UNDERSTANDING THE WHY BEHIND MY HURT

When I was a young girl, I was reserved and shy around boys, even though I had an underlying curiosity about them. Sure, I had friends who were boys, but our interactions never went beyond mere friendship, and I was content with that. Yet, deep down, I held a belief that I was more like the beast than the beauty, convinced that no guy would ever see me as wife material. Whenever I was teased about boys, it increased my self-consciousness, fostering embarrassment and shame. This led to a persistent belief that I might never find a partner and reinforced the notion that I wasn't deserving of love and affection. One more scar. Consequently, I wrestled with issues of identity and worth and, at times, wondered if I would possibly compromise my integrity just to experience what I thought might be love. As with most revelations, I wasn't aware of how deep this wound went, the shame of being different and not being as beautiful as I thought was necessary to be worth loving. As I reflect, I see how this false belief born from a scar impacted the way I approached relationships with boys during my teenage years.

Deep down in my heart, I wanted to find "the one" who would love me unconditionally. Ever since I had written in my diary what I specifically wanted in a guy, I began praying that I would not have to compromise but that God would give me my heart's desire.

I found myself, fresh from an extreme makeover, settling into my new life as a high school student in the Valley. Unexpectedly, I began to notice a shift in attention from guys. It caught me off guard to realize that guys were showing interest in me beyond mere friendship. They were drawn to fun, down-to-earth girls, and I fit that description for them. I didn't know how to respond or what to do with the new attention. So, awkwardly, in those early relationships, I resorted to kissing guys quickly because I thought that's what you're supposed to do when a guy likes you, right? I mean, that's what I saw in the movies and on TV. It became my default action, without any real affection or a deep connection with these boys. This was my protection response born out of scars that had piled up. I wasn't thrilled with my actions but it's what I believed was needed in order to not lose the newfound attention I was receiving or have a guy not like me anymore. During the Cornerstone tour, not only was I interested in Nate but I was currently in a "relationship" with a guy who would soon be moving away. And there was a third guy on the tour that I knew had feelings for me. My heart soon found itself being pulled in three different directions. Embarrassingly, I made the decision to show attention to all of them. This became quite ridiculous when I found myself holding hands with two different guys while watching the same movie! I know, I know. What on earth was I thinking? Obviously, I really wasn't thinking. This feeling stemmed from a deep fear of letting others down, a fear of saying no because I knew firsthand the pain of rejection. After Nate and I shared that quick kiss on the bus, we returned home, and it soon felt as though the tour had become a distant memory that rapidly faded. Nate found out that I had kissed someone else on the tour, and he was heartbroken and understandably upset. I couldn't blame him. However, I was quite unsure about my feelings and what I really wanted. When school started back, the one "boyfriend" ended up moving as was expected, and the other guy from the tour relocated with his family to Houston six months later.

Rumors spread and on the first day of school, I was approached by girls who questioned whether it was true that Nate and the other guy from our school had an interest in me—or worse, if I had feelings for them. Although I remained silent, it became clear that I had unwittingly stumbled into the territory of "mean girls."

That fall, my dad decided to use his gift of teaching and knowledge of the Bible to teach at VCS, which allowed me to feel safe. Dad, the amazing fun teacher, quickly became everyone's favorite and everyone loved him, and I mean everyone. Then things took a toxic turn, whether due to jealousy or an offense I had committed. I suspected some kids in my class were making fun of me. I had dealt with teasing before, but I genuinely never thought it would get as bad as it did. Three "mean girls" walked around, yelling "Scarface." They also coughed and said it in class, and soon many of the kids joined in.

I eventually gathered the courage to ask the "mean girls" if they were making fun of me, and they casually replied, "Oh no, it's just an inside joke." I tried to brush it off, though I couldn't help but feel self-conscious. This uncertainty fed into my insecurities and created a wound that I wasn't even sure would be able to scar. Years later, after graduation, one of the three "mean girls" came to me with an apology and spilled the beans. She explained how "Scarface" was indeed a reference to me and confessed how they raided my locker and took a few things. I felt a mix of frustration at hearing this and gratitude for her honesty. It is accurate that eventually the truth will be revealed.

Despite how traumatic and awful my high school experience was, I must confess, I was no angel. Outwardly, I presented myself as someone I wasn't. I still had my set of inward scars; they just looked different. I was definitely judgmental about various individuals, convinced that my criticisms were justified. Pridefully, I found it much easier to identify flaws in others, while struggling to acknowledge my own shortcomings.

Nate was guarded and did not have much to do with me for another year. I understood. Yet, deep down, I felt like—or hopefully wished—there was an unrelenting force drawing us together. Nate and I slowly started talking again, and we began to rekindle our friendship to the point of becoming isolated with one another, as neither one of us had any other really close friendships. Initially, I don't think we had the intention of isolating ourselves from others. However, being at that particular school, where there was a lot of negativity and "mean girl" behavior, the isolation seemed to happen naturally. At first, it felt like we were pushed into it, causing an us-versus-them dichotomy, which was not healthy. Though others saw us as kind and godly kids who didn't drink or do drugs, the perception of us didn't exactly align with how we were living our lives either. We began our journey together, starting with early morning Bible studies before school. But, even with the best of intentions, it seemed that our drive-in movie experiences evolved to be less about the movie and more about each other. From that point, we pushed the boundaries until there were none left to push.

Looking back, I completely understand the allure of keeping "stuff" hidden from everyone, concealing it behind closed doors. It had an element of excitement all on its own, and we became quite skilled at being hidden. Or so we thought—but the Lord knew.

CHAPTER TWELVE

Wake-Up Call

Soon after we moved to the Valley, I had the opportunity of a lifetime. My best friend, Jessica, from my former school in Dallas, asked me if I wanted to travel with her and her parents, who were evangelists known around the world, to Australia in June 1997. "Finally," I thought to myself, "I have waited my whole life (a whole fourteen years) to start fulfilling my calling to travel around the world and share my story that God is real and still performs miracles today." This journey wouldn't just be a plane ride to a country far away; it would also be an adventure that would happen only with divine intervention.

While this opportunity was extremely exciting, over the course of my life, my parents had spent thousands of dollars working on finalizing my adoption paperwork with Guatemalan and US lawyers in order to get my US citizenship. In 1994, my parents were able to secure a social security number for me. When inquiring about citizenship, a lawyer told my parents that I was in the "system" and that's all I needed. So when it came time for me to get my passport, my parents figured they only needed to file the passport paperwork, and I would be good to go. Little did we know, this was completely untrue, and my passport was denied. The State Department blamed our Houston lawyer for neglecting vital paperwork, and that is when my parents realized this lawyer was only taking more and more money without actually filing any of the actual paperwork. So they contacted another lawyer in Houston who would get everything in order, but he came with another hefty fee of $1,500. This new lawyer, who spoke just a little English, called my parents often to probe into the depths of my story. The frustration levels skyrocketed for my parents, given that the requested information had already been eloquently laid out in the paperwork they initially gave. The singular task entrusted to this lawyer was to expedite the delivery of my paperwork to the State Department within the golden ninety-day window. My parents contacted the lawyer well past the ninety days and were greeted not with success or progress but with the deafening echoes of silence.

May had arrived, and with only one month left before my scheduled departure, my parents still hadn't received any additional information from the lawyer in Houston. Out of desperation, my dad reached out to the House of Representative's office and spoke with a woman named Norma, who proved to be very knowledgeable and helpful. She inquired whether my parents could be at the immigration office the next Tuesday. Without hesitation, my parents emphatically said they'd be there.

Tuesday arrived, and the immigration office was buzzing with a swarm of individuals trying to get their essential documentation. My parents went to grab a number, and oddly, they were instructed not to. Instead, they were directed to simply take a seat. Hours passed. The day was almost over, and everyone else had been served. Baffled, my parents approached the front office, seeking answers. The woman they spoke with dropped a bombshell—my paperwork was nowhere to be found! A swift decision was made: a return on the following Thursday was requested, this time with my parents' high school transcripts, marriage license, taxes from the previous ten years, and, naturally, me. The laundry list of demands left my parents dumbfounded. They had everything packed, on the cusp of moving to a new home, and making the quest for a decade's worth of tax documents felt to them like it was akin to finding the ark of the covenant.

    Miraculously, Mom remembered having labeled the tax box with a blue lid, so they quickly located it. My mom's mother, Grandma Dot, who lived in Washington State, drove to Bellingham High School and obtained and sent my parents' high school transcripts via overnight mail. This was another miracle because this was before the days of email and only a few days away from my trip to Australia.

    Initially, one lawyer advised my dad that all of my Guatemalan documents needed to be professionally translated into English. However, upon reaching the translation service, he encountered a woman who suggested otherwise. She informed him that translating all the paperwork would be excessively costly, amounting to thousands of dollars. Instead, she proposed reading through some of the documents and condensing them to two pages, which would cost a total of twenty dollars.

When my parents visited the immigration office in Hidalgo County that Thursday, with all the requested documents and me, it turned out that the translation was indeed unnecessary because Mr. Hinajosa, the official handling my paperwork, could read Spanish. After about fifteen minutes of perusing my documents, he informed my parents that the use of an incorrect form had been the reason for the complications. We were all frustrated and concerned since I only had three days before my scheduled departure, but luckily Mr. Hinajosa made a phone call and arranged for the correct form, charging only ninety dollars for the correct document.

Mr. Hinajosa sat in front of my parents, his hands resting on a thick manila folder. My parents nervously fidgeted with their paperwork, hoping that everything was in order for my temporary citizenship to Australia. Mr. Hinajosa passed my parents a piece of white paper, but it wasn't the expected document—it was my permanent citizenship! Overjoyed and relieved, they quickly contacted the Australian government and provided my passport number. Three days later, in June 1997, I received my visa to Australia—nothing short of a true miracle.

DOWN UNDER

Australia exceeded all my expectations and captured my imagination. As our private helicopter soared over the Gold Coast, I pressed my face against the window and marveled at the endless expanse of green below. Wallabies hopped in a graceful rhythm, their muscular legs propelling them forward as far as my eyes could reach, until my eyes met the ocean. The excitement continued as I had my first scuba diving experience in the Great Barrier Reef. However, as I descended into the water and felt the weight of the oxygen tank on my back, panic set in. I struggled to breathe and quickly resurfaced multiple times, gasping for air. Just as I was about to give up, my instructor realized he had forgotten to open my oxygen valve. Relief flooded over me as I finally took deep breaths and continued my underwater adventure with newfound determination. Australia continued to exceed all expectations and capture my imagination with its stunning natural beauty. During our visit, we encountered a barracuda and even had the opportunity to pet it, though that was an easy pass for me, but I did get close. Our trip took us from Sydney up through the entire Gold Coast, and it was filled with one unforgettable moment after another.

During my trip, I had the incredible opportunity to attend a Sunday service at Hillsong Church. Upon entering the building, we saw the evangelist being greeted warmly by members of the congregation. My heart swelled with pride as he took the stage to deliver a powerful message filled with passion and grace.

The pastor went out of his way to ask if we could have breakfast with none other than Darlene Zschech, a world-renowned Christian worship leader and singer-songwriter from Hillsong Church. She is my all-time favorite worship leader whom I've admired since a young age. She exuded humility and kindness as she greeted us with a warm smile and hug. I was in awe of her talent and humbled by her presence. As we sat down to eat, my usually talkative self was momentarily speechless, soaking in every word she shared about her heart and call to serve through music. It was a moment I will always cherish.

Jessica and her family proved to be the most gracious hosts, ensuring our time in Australia was nothing short of miraculous. The memories created during this trip are etched in my heart, leaving a mark that whispers of future return visits. Australia, with its breathtaking landscapes and genuine love from such kind people, became more than a destination—it became a place I knew I would revisit one day.

RECORD DEAL

Once I was back from my Australian adventure, an exciting opportunity opened up for me. I was offered the financial backing to go to Nashville, Tennessee, and record my solo debut album. As a teenager, I felt I had hit the music "jackpot," a real game-changer in my long-awaited musical career. Amazement flooded over me as I watched these doors of opportunity swing wide open. Accompanied by my brother-in-law, Jay, my mom and I drove to Nashville to meet with high-profile producers.

When we stepped into their basement studio at 10:00 a.m., the producers acted like they had just woken up, surrounded by open whiskey bottles. They explained that whiskey helped them with their vocals in the morning. Undeterred, I confidently belted out "How Great Thou Art" in full voice, feeling like I'd aced my audition. The producers were encouraging but they also appeared rather indifferent. They shared a couple of songs that left me unsure about the musical direction they proposed, as I did not feel the two songs they pitched were my style. Back home from visiting the Sound Kitchen Studio that day, we were all excited about what lay ahead. But, much to our dismay, the stock market decided to do a nosedive, and bam, just like that, all my financial support vanished into thin air as though it never existed. The only way to move forward with the record was to pay eighty thousand dollars out of my own pocket, a sum neither my parents nor I had stashed away under the couch cushions.

Within the span of less than a month, I heard both songs that the producers had presented to me playing on our local Christian radio station. One song was performed by a music group with phenomenal harmonies, and the other by a young girl my age with an incredibly soulful, powerful voice and vocal range. That day, I received the scar of disappointment, my dreams of pursuing a music career slipping through my fingers. My hands were tied, and I could do nothing about it except watch another young girl pass me by and only hope for and dream of another opportunity someday—but another opportunity never presented itself. I couldn't understand why God would allow something that was just within arm's reach to be taken away. Only now, with years of experience, can I discern the protective hand of the Lord. Life's funny that way, isn't it?

BACK AGAIN

My first trip to Australia had captivated me, and then again at seventeen years of age, I received another amazing opportunity to travel back to Australia! This time, I would be going with a world-renowned female speaker, Katie. Although we'd never met in person, she'd heard my story and was deeply moved, so she invited me to accompany her and share my experiences while exploring the Perth side of Australia. In addition, we would conclude our trip by traveling to Singapore. My response was an emphatic yes, and I was incredibly excited about this unbelievable opportunity.

This part of the story is quite humorous, and I can't help but chuckle when I think back about the day Katie and I met. I showed up to the airport wearing overalls and a snug pink shirt, with my hair in curls pulled up on top of my head in a high ponytail. Meanwhile, Katie looked like she had just stepped off a magazine cover. She looked stunning in high heels, a beautifully tailored suit, perfectly straight hair, and just the right amount of makeup to enhance her natural beauty. From her first glance, observing me from the top of my head to my Converse high-top shoes, it seemed she might have been second-guessing inviting me along for this adventure with her. But I was simply thrilled about the journey ahead.

We hit it off during the flight, discussing life, relationships, and makeup, and she shared a tip about taking Tylenol PM for long flights, which I tried and found effective. It was pretty late upon our arrival in Australia, and we didn't have a hotel reservation for the night. Katie approached our taxi driver and asked if he could take us to a safe, nice hotel, and he assured us he had the perfect one in mind.

As we pulled up to the hotel, it was dark, and we noticed the high rise but couldn't tell anything was amiss. When we got out of the cab, the driver helped us with our luggage, and he sped away quickly. While I didn't think much of it, I could tell that Katie was hesitant. When we entered our hotel room, I didn't initially notice anything wrong compared to some of the places I'd been to in the Valley, but when Katie turned on the faucet, an unexpected guest scurried out—a cockroach emerged along with murky brown water. We let out simultaneous screams and dashed to the safety of the bed, believing the roach could not reach us. At this point, Katie had already had enough and began making quick calls; the hotel was clearly not acceptable. In my opinion, the roach and the brown water were deal-breakers, so I felt relieved knowing Katie was going to change our plans and get us out of this less-than-ideal situation.

I'm not exactly sure how she did it, but Katie arranged for us to stay at another hotel, one that was more in line with what she was initially expecting—a luxurious five-star establishment, and I was all for it.

While speaking at schools, everything unfolded smoothly and seamlessly. Katie delivered impactful speeches on abstinence from sex until marriage and sexually transmitted diseases and employed analogies that related to young people. Her eloquence and charm garnered admiration from everyone who listened. Likewise, I received a warm reception as I shared my personal testimony of how God miraculously saved my life through adoption, defying medical odds, and giving me a voice to sing. The kids always enjoyed ending on a high note by joining me in dancing and singing a techno song.

As we continued exploring and speaking at various schools, we eventually crossed paths along our route with one of the largest churches in Perth. It was there that I discovered Katie had been in a long-distance relationship with the pastor's son. So we stayed at Katie's boyfriend's luxurious condo, which was incredibly modern and high-tech, far different from anything I'd ever seen back in the States.

We attended a service, and Katie's boyfriend asked me if I would be willing to lead worship the next day. I was comfortable with singing a song, but leading worship was outside my comfort zone so I declined the opportunity, especially after hearing the remarkable talent of the worship team. Their sound seemed to exude a level of talent that surpassed even the likes of Hillsong but with an added touch of soul. I was truly in awe.

We left Australia and boarded another flight that took us to Singapore. After settling in, I noticed that our room had a connecting door to another one, but I didn't think much of it at the time.

Later that evening, a loud, heavy knock sounded on our door. Scared, Katie looked through the peephole but answered when she recognized the voice on the other side. It turned out that her boyfriend had taken a separate flight to surprise Katie to spend time with her and had booked the room connected to ours. This was such a sweet moment for them, but by this point in our trip, it only escalated an underlying tension that had developed between Katie and me. I wasn't just feeling like a third wheel; I was undeniably a third wheel.

The original plan was that Katie and I were supposed to meet up with Bob, a pastor and a prophet from Singapore, the following day. But now that Katie and her boyfriend were together, they kindly explained to me they were planning a visit to the zoo the next day. They hesitantly suggested that I could join them if I wanted to, but I knew they were also looking forward to some time alone. That meant

I would be spending time alone with a pastor from Singapore named Bob, whom I had never met before.

Katie and her boyfriend were out late that evening having dinner and I had fallen asleep. Suddenly I was awakened by loud banging coming from the door connecting our rooms. I wasn't sure of the exact time, but it was very early the next morning. I hesitated to open the door until I heard someone calling my name, "Camey, open the door—open the door right now!"

When I opened the door, I was met by a visibly upset Katie. She questioned why I had locked the door. Confused, I responded that I didn't remember locking it and had no idea what was going on. I was utterly confused. As I lay on the bed now wide awake, I couldn't help but feel a bit upset about how I'd been treated. It seemed that Katie and her boyfriend might have been intimate, considering the early knocking on the door and her somewhat embarrassed and upset demeanor. I lay back down and put the pieces together, contemplating what had just happened. All I could conclude was that Katie was not living what she was preaching.

YOU'VE GOT MAIL

The following day, Katie and her boyfriend were preparing to leave for the zoo, and I distinctly remember descending the stairs to the hotel lobby alone, where I encountered a man standing by the glass doors. As Katie rushed by, she briefly introduced me to Bob, then she and her boyfriend ran to catch their cab. "Camey," he said, smiling and reaching out to shake my hand, "it's nice to meet you.

I'm Bob." But the words he spoke next left me with my mouth wide open: "The thoughts you had walking down the stairs about Katie being a hypocrite, right now, are accurate; you're not wrong." He had read my mind because those were precisely the thoughts I had as I'd descended the stairs. While I had some knowledge of prophecy, this was remarkably specific. It felt like a breath of fresh air and relief to know that what I had been thinking about Katie was confirmed. In that moment, I knew Bob was a man of God, a prophet, and I could feel safe in his presence without fear.

We got into Bob's car, and he asked me what I'd like to see in Singapore. I felt so honored and special, but also felt undeserving that he was taking time out of his day to spend time with me, since originally Katie and I had been scheduled to meet with him. He suggested going to the zoo, but I informed him that Katie and her boyfriend were already there, so that idea was tabled. Then, he proposed visiting the botanical gardens in Singapore, known for its beautiful flowers. Not having a strong preference, I agreed.

While Bob and I were there, we strolled around, engaging in conversation as he shared details about his family and why they couldn't be with him at the moment. He also discussed his faith and Christianity, as well as his church in Singapore and how it was not like churches in the States or even in Australia. He mentioned that owning a car and a home in Singapore was a significant accomplishment, suggesting he might have been a successful businessman. Our conversation touched on my parents' ministry and life in general.

After a leisurely stroll through the breathtaking gardens, Bob and I sat down on a stone bench to take a break. While chatting about our favorite flowers and plants, our stomachs grumbled, reminding us that it was lunchtime. Bob asked me my food preference, and being an American, I knew pizza was always a safe option, so that is what I suggested. He took me to an underground pizza joint that felt exclusive and secretive as if you had to be "in the know" to gain entry. There, in the midst of the clandestine atmosphere, with only us present at first, he told me to order anything I wanted, assuring me nothing was off-limits. Looking at the menu, I was in awe of all the options ranging from classic pepperoni to more exotic toppings like truffles and caviar. And they had especially attentive service and a flawless standard that ensured every detail was impeccably managed. It seemed as though the staff catered to Bob with a familiarity that suggested they knew him well.

After a few minutes, Bob's friend, a robust gentleman, joined us for lunch, his attention fully captured by Bob's every word. I couldn't help but think that Bob's friend could easily be mistaken for a bouncer at a club, and a wave of disorientation swept over me, prompting the thought, "I'm certainly not in Texas anymore." The best way I can describe this underground pizza joint was undeniably posh, yet it carried a sort of mafia-style ambiance, even though my logical side knew better.

Despite being in a place entirely new to me, I felt safe with Bob and his friend. The food, prepared in an open stove oven, was nothing short of amazing—a culinary experience unlike anything I'd encountered in the States. Following our delectable pizza meal, Bob mentioned that he needed to pick something up at his house, so we headed there next.

Upon arrival, we found ourselves at a multistory home, certainly very nice, but not overly grand. Yet, in the context of Singapore's housing standards, his home was considered upscale and impressive, well worth more than a million dollars in our currency.

Sitting on his couch for a brief moment, my mind wandered. He had stepped away to grab some water, leaving me alone with my thoughts. I wondered how my parents would react to my being in this situation. It wasn't that I felt threatened or in danger—if harm were on his agenda, I'd have been a goner, but rather just the idea of being alone with a man.

Perhaps they might not approve; I was uncertain. But then there was Bob, the gracious host, breaking through the tension as he handed me a glass of water. It was like he could sense my discomfort, and with genuine warmth, he dove into some light conversation upon his return, instantly easing the unease that had momentarily clouded the room.

In the midst of our conversation, my gaze was captivated by a glass coffee table filled with hundreds of turtles—some small, others large. Now that I had a conversation starter, he shared that these turtles held a special place in his wife's heart. Though I wasn't entirely certain why, it seemed that our discussion about these charming creatures was the segue, and Bob turned to me with compassion and love in his eyes, speaking to something much deeper in my heart. Something that I thought was concealed and hidden. "You and Nate were caught in a compromising situation by your sister."

I gazed at him, confusion etched across my face. He said he could go into further specific details if I'd like, but I quietly declined, acknowledging the undeniable truth of his words. There was no need to continue. What he said next was both encouraging and perplexing. God had great plans, but Nate and I were unequally yoked.

In that moment I became a digital computer, processing everything he was saying and attempting to piece it all together. Questions raced through my mind: What does this all mean? Should I end things with Nate? I didn't want to, but I needed to make sense of it all. Amid the mental chaos, compassion and love flooded my being, and I realized that God was speaking directly to my heart. Bob was right—I hadn't been living right. Conviction washed over me; I acknowledged I was wrong.

Our next stop was at Bob's church, and stepping inside felt strangely reminiscent of my dad's church, Cornerstone Community Church in Roanoke. The sanctuary was approximately the same size and painted in a matching color, and warm lighting cast a pleasant ambiance. At the front, a cross hung on the wall, with a wooden pulpit in the front. Bob mentioned that although the church might seem small, it had recently undergone remodeling and was considered a significant-sized church in Singapore, probably one of the largest churches in this region.

Bob proudly gave me a tour of their newly remodeled church and introduced me to another one of his friends. The moment I met this gentleman, it became apparent that he too was a mighty man of God. Bob then led us to another room with windows overlooking the sanctuary, possibly a space where mothers brought their young children. The three of us sat in chairs beside each other in a triangle, and Bob once again spoke of the calling on my life, revealing that I was called to be a prophetic psalmist. However, the term was unfamiliar to me, and all I could envision was King David from the Bible playing his harp before Saul—an image that didn't seem particularly enjoyable.

Despite my initial reservations, my curiosity was piqued. Bob extended an invitation for me to pray, sing, or share whatever the Lord laid on my heart. In that moment, a wave of shock overwhelmed me, as if my brain was struggling to process everything unfolding before my eyes.

The two men began to pray fervently, moving back and forth and possibly even speaking in a different language. It was at that very moment that I felt completely out of my element, as it had been years since I had actively engaged with the charismatic and spiritual aspects of my faith because my current school was the complete opposite of charismatic. This was a far cry from the last time I'd experienced such things when I was younger.

They asked me to sing and to join in, but it felt as though my vocal cords were paralyzed. I was hesitant, fearing that if I did sing, I would be off-key since they were each singing on entirely different notes, and I didn't know where to come in. In hindsight, I realized that they weren't concerned about how I sounded; they were simply encouraging me to bring forth the dormant gift that lay inside of me. I was overwhelmed with gratitude for their presence and the time they had shared with me. I wasn't sure how God was moving, but I knew something was stirring and changing within me. I was a changed person, and to this day, I am in awe of how God allowed me to meet such a mighty man of God.

Once I returned home, everything moved like a whirlwind. Truthfully, I didn't really want to break up with Nate, but I knew something had to change, so I did. It was short-lived, though, because not long after the breakup, we found ourselves back together as if nothing had happened. I did mention to Nate what Bob had said about us being unequally yoked, and this infuriated him. He questioned Bob, saying, "Who is this guy to judge my heart?"

For several months, I was torn about whether Nate and I should be together or not. Eventually, I wrote a somewhat chaotic email to Bob, looking for more specific answers. His reply was brief and his main point was "Seek God and He will direct your heart." Even though I was wanting a step-by-step instruction, what he said was all I needed.

Bob had altered the course of my life in more ways than I ever could have realized back then. His words weren't just spoken; they held weight and I knew they would come to pass.

A LOOSE SCREW

It was around this time that I decided to stay with my sister in the Dallas-Fort Worth area to help babysit her kids. One day, while absentmindedly running my tongue over my gums, I made an unsettling discovery. A strange hole seemed to be forming in the upper region of my gums. At first glimpse, all I could make out was a shiny, round object, and I hadn't the faintest idea what it might be. As weeks went by, it dawned on me that this mysterious protrusion was something metal. I felt a rising terror welling up inside and feared that my mouth was quite literally falling apart at the seams — and worried that another unwanted surgery loomed ahead. Paranoia even led me to wonder if I had contracted some rare gum disease.

After putting it off for far too long, I finally mustered the courage to schedule an appointment with Dr. Hobar. Since my parents were still in the Valley, my sister Shannon accompanied me, and although I was eager to see Dr. Hobar, I didn't want this to be the reason we met again.

Dr. Hobar swiftly confirmed my deepest suspicion—I actually had a "screw loose." It seemed almost too ironic, as I'd always felt like something was off within me—but now it was a tangible reality. I literally had a loose screw. The doctor informed me that the hardware would need to be removed. Initially, I thought he was referring to a later time, but when I asked when, he responded, "Today. It will only take a minute." I thought, I don't want to go through this. Then again, how much longer could I keep ignoring it?

He assured me that removing the screw would be painless and that I should only feel just a little bit of pressure. As Dr. Hobar excused himself from the examination room, I could no longer keep my fears and anxieties bottled up and tears began streaming down my face, releasing a torrent of pent-up emotions. Shannon came near and offered comforting words, reassuring me that it was all right to cry. I saw tears welling up in her own eyes, helping me feel less alone and embarrassed by my vulnerability.

Dr. Hobar returned, with a sterile screwdriver in hand, and I braced myself for the worst, recalling the excruciating memory of having wires removed after surgery. To my surprise, the discomfort was minimal, nothing like what I'd imagined. Dr. Hobar's words had rung true—it was painless, aside from a slight sensation of pressure. And just like that, the small screw rested in Dr. Hobar's palm as I was left alive and ready to face another day.

HEART ATTACK

As a child I had horrible, terrorizing nightmares in which I would have to choose and watch one set of my parents die, either my biological parents or adoptive parents. These dreams were a mix of the issues surrounding adoption and the fact that my parents were a few years older than most of my friends' parents at school. While I wasn't embarrassed by this, I did worry about their deaths. These dreams were traumatizing, but since they dealt, in part, with issues surrounding adoption, I never told my parents about them, as I didn't want them to feel bad. This was one more scar created by fear of the unknown. I remember praying, "Lord, give my parents a long life, and let them be here when I turn forty." I remember begging the Lord for this request.

It wouldn't be until I was much older, in my thirties, that I would grasp the faith that Heaven is real. Once I understood that the transition from this life to Heaven is, in fact, more real than the physical world we live in, death no longer held me by fear.

But, when I was in high school, I was still very much afraid of death. I knew that my mom's dad passed away in his mid-forties from a heart attack, and my mom frequently visited doctors concerning her blood pressure and heart productivity. Her blood pressure was consistently high, but her pulse remained quite low. However, she was always active and determined and never allowed her health to hinder her. I didn't think she was unaware or in denial, but rather, she refused to let anything impede her serving the Lord.

I was also aware that my dad had some blood pressure and cholesterol issues. While I was in high school, my dad was on the court during the heated staff versus student basketball game, wearing a headband and wristbands that gave him a comical appearance. Suddenly, he stopped in his tracks, bent over in discomfort, and signaled for a substitute to take his place. It was unlike anything I'd ever seen from my typically strong and gentle giant of a dad. I wanted to shout for the game to stop and even mentioned to Nate that something was not right with Dad. I vaguely recall going over to check on him, but he assured me he was okay and returned to the game for a brief moment before coming back out again.

We later went to the hospital, and I sat nervously in the waiting room with my mom by my side. This time, it was my dad who was undergoing a medical procedure—a heart catheterization. I watched as he was wheeled away on a stretcher, his normally strong stature looking small and vulnerable in the sterile environment. Tears streamed down my face as I thought about all the times he'd taken care of me when I was in the hospital. Now, it was my turn to feel helpless, with the only action I could take being to pray for his well-being. Mom shared my worries, trying to hold back tears as we waited for what felt like an eternity. I couldn't shake the feeling of dread that something could go wrong. It wasn't until years later, after studying nursing, that I learned a heart catheterization is a routine procedure, rarely with complications, but at that time, I had no idea.

After what seemed like hours, the doctor finally emerged from the operating room. His tired face broke into a smile as he approached us and said, "Rea is in recovery and doing well. He'll need three stents, which we can put in tomorrow." Relief washed over us, lifting the invisible weight from our shoulders. The doctor went on to explain that during the basketball game, my dad had suffered a heart attack and the lower part of his heart was not functioning properly. Thankfully, the doctor was confident that a few stents would be sufficient to address the issue.

REUNION

After my dad experienced a heart attack in the year 2000, I became aware that Jesús, my biological father, was also aging and facing his own health challenges. Despite my parents' ongoing encouragement for me to eventually meet Rita and Jesús, I typically dismissed the idea, placing it in the back of my mind. However, after my dad's heart attack, I wondered what would happen if Jesús passed away, and I never expressed my gratitude for all he did to keep me alive. I didn't want to live with regrets.

Now that my paperwork was complete and I had my passport, I found that I didn't want to entertain the "what ifs." To my parents' surprise, I said I wanted to go and visit.

Dad was given standby tickets from a pilot who was a member at our previous church. Approaching Guatemala City on the airplane, I started to get butterflies in my stomach. Had I made the right choice? As soon as we landed, I immediately wanted to turn around. My stomach was in knots, and I kept asking, "Why did I come here?"

I wasn't entirely sure of the exact plan, which I didn't like, because I prefer to know what's going on. The other challenge was the language barrier; I only knew a few words in Spanish that I'd learned in high school. Fortunately, Dad, who attended language school and my biological brother Umberto, who knew some English, became my official translators.

As we drove through the winding roads of the mountains, the anticipation in the car was palpable. Instead of arriving at the house in the mountains that had been described to me, we pulled up to Umberto's house in Salamá. My heart raced as I saw a crowd of people outside. A film crew was there with bright lights and cameras, adding to the already chaotic scene. If I had been nervous before, I was then on another level. Upon walking through the door, I kept a close eye on my dad since I didn't know anyone there. The room was filled with beautiful, unfamiliar faces, all looking at us with curiosity. Then, among the sea of strangers, I spotted Rita, my biological mother, whom I recognized from pictures. She stood out with her short stature and hazel eyes that mirrored my own. Her skin was a beautiful light brown, unlike my own darker complexion, and her curly black hair cascaded down past her shoulders. Frozen and overwhelmed with emotions, she came toward me and pulled me into a tight embrace, tears streaming down her face. "Mi amore . . . mi bebé," she whispered through sobs. It was hard to believe that the last time she had seen me, I was just a newborn—now here I stood before her, a nineteen-year-old woman.

I was in a state of shock in every sense. The overwhelming moment left me with no specific emotion—I was not overjoyed, sad, happy, mad, or upset. I was numb. I knew my face was not showing any emotion, and in what I thought was an act of kindness, I made myself cry to let them know that I cared and was feeling something. I smiled and greeted almost everyone with a kiss on the cheek and a hug, which was different from the way I typically greeted people, but I was appreciative of their lovingness, thoughtfulness, and willingness to make me feel loved and special. I kept looking around to find my dad. I wanted to maintain contact with him because I was concerned that the reunion might unintentionally hurt his feelings. I didn't want Dad to believe he wasn't good enough; it was quite the opposite. He was my one and only true dad, and no one could ever replace him. The notion of searching for a "real" dad was the furthest thing from the truth because I had already found my real dad—James Rea Thompson. He had chosen me.

I don't believe my dad was actually feeling what I was concerned about, but that was my internal battle. I finally saw him, not making much noise, standing out of the way against the wall; I guess he thought he needed to not intrude on my experience. Personally, I wouldn't have minded; his intrusion would have been gladly received. As happy as everyone was, it was an awkward experience for me. I knew most of them were blood-related, but I didn't know them, and these lovely people were as foreign to me as I was to them.

As I prepared to leave Guatemalan soil and return home, I was again surrounded by these warm, loving people. Their deep love for family and their rich cultural heritage radiated from every conversation and interaction. It made me proud to know that I shared this heritage with them. Yet, as I looked around, I realized that while my life had continued as usual, their lives were marked by the absence of a child, a reality I couldn't fully comprehend.

This reunion was an emotional one that they had anticipated for years. They loved me, held me dear in their hearts, and lamented my absence. However, my perspective was different. I didn't know them personally, had not seen them for nearly two decades, and only knew them through stories I'd been told. I was raised thousands of miles away by a kind and loving man and woman, people I called Mom and Dad.

PART II

CHAPTER THIRTEEN

Not Happily Ever After

After high school, my original plan was to return to the DFW area to be closer to my family and friends. Nate, in the hope of us being closer during college, decided to attend Dallas Baptist University. However, due to both of my parents facing health challenges, I decided to stay in the Valley and complete my basic college courses at the University of Texas in Edinburg. I knew I needed to attend college, but I really didn't know what I wanted to study at that time.

After two years into my basics and two years into a long-distance relationship, I received a call from Nate expressing, in a kind, yet urgent way, "We have to figure something out soon or this long-distance relationship won't work." Without hesitation, I packed my bags the next day and, in a whirlwind, decided to attend Baylor School of Nursing in Dallas. The school year had already begun, but I was determined to catch up and make it work. By then, I was living on my own, navigating living arrangements, and budgeting for tuition and expenses as I pursued my dream career.

One day, the phone rang, and two familiar voices greeted me on the other end—it was Dr. Hobar and his wife, Robin. They generously offered me the opportunity to live in their back house in Highland Park, one of the most prestigious areas of Texas. It was a beautiful, fully furnished two-bedroom home located just a few blocks from nursing school, and it was rent-free! Dr. Hobar had rescued me as a little girl, and now, as my dream had foretold, he was coming to my rescue once again.

Everything seemed to be working perfectly—or so I thought. I was working as a nurse extern at a downtown hospital, where I had the privilege of holding people's hearts during open heart surgery. Nursing school presented its own set of challenges, dealing with instructors whom I felt were determined not to let me graduate. Though I never failed a class, it was difficult. However, nursing school turned out not to be the only obstacle I would encounter. Nate and I had been dating for a total of five years. And this individual who had been my steadfast companion through the highs and lows, someone I considered the safest, kindest, smartest, most trustworthy and godly person I knew, was concealing a secret. Nate was looking at pornography, something I never thought he would do. I recognize that everyone faces temptation and no one is perfect, and while this might not be significant for some, this revelation hit me harder than I expected.

It wasn't just about him seeing the images. The deception, manipulation, and gaslighting hurt the most. He had a way of twisting my words until I felt like I was losing my mind, leading me down rabbit holes where he could always come out on top. How could someone who claimed to love me do this? How many more secrets were lurking behind his charming smile? My mind struggled to comprehend the full impact of his actions and what they could mean for our relationship going forward. He downplayed the harm, but could I even believe anything he said to me anymore?

I felt betrayed and didn't know whom to turn to for support. The knowledge of him lusting after other women made me doubt myself again and question whether I was enough for him in terms of my appearance. Throughout my entire life, I have dealt with these thoughts: Am I sufficient for you, am I attractive enough, and am I deserving of love?

Despite Nate's repeated assurances that it was a one-time mistake, I couldn't shake the feeling of betrayal and hurt every time I stumbled upon yet another pornographic image on his computer. Each time, I was met with an excuse as to how the pornography mysteriously appeared on his computer. He claimed it wasn't a problem for him, and I desperately wanted to believe that was true, but deep down I knew it was a problem. Those answers appeased me temporarily, as we both believed that once we were married, things would improve.

Nate proposed during our junior year of college, and we set the date for our wedding: August 16, 2003. As our wedding day approached, my mom, my sister-in-law Leslie, and sisters worked tirelessly to prepare for the big day, assisting with decorations, venue, food, invitations, and helping financially. We sent out four hundred invitations, and everything seemed perfectly in order. However, two nights before the wedding, while on Nate's computer scrolling through music options for our reception playlist, I stumbled upon a link that required a password. It wasn't my intention to invade his privacy, but curiosity got the better of me, and I used the password he'd given me for computer access.

Upon opening the link, I was overwhelmed by what I discovered—pornography videos, chats, pictures—a flood of emotions hit me all at once. I went through a moment of denial, followed by anger, bargaining, hurt, sadness, and, primarily, shock. I was totally out of control of what was unfolding before me. When I confronted Nate in a fury of anger, he denied any connection to the content. However, when I mentioned using his password, he was left speechless, unsure of how to respond. At that moment, the scar of betrayal and rejection was etched upon my heart. I felt deeply hurt, and I expressed my pain through anger, convinced that I had the right to feel justified in these intense emotions.

I finally realized the gravity of the situation. Nate had an addiction. It felt as though God were presenting me with a choice—to address this significant issue or proceed with the wedding, knowing what lay ahead. I wrestled with the decision of canceling the wedding, and facing potential embarrassment was daunting. I struggled with the fear of disappointing everyone who had invested in our wedding, including out-of-town guests with booked flights. I also knew that canceling would probably end our relationship, and I deeply, truly loved him with my whole heart. I also had a deep-seated root of fear and rejection, believing no other man would ever accept me based on both my physical and internal scars. I truly thought I was too hideous for anyone to love more than a friend. Ultimately, I chose to proceed with the marriage, but the words of Bob in Singapore rang in my mind: "You and Nate are unequally yoked."

Dad, wearing his black robe with a stole, stood at my side, ready to escort me to the front before officiating my wedding. He turned to me and looked into my eyes, whispering, "Camey, are you sure you are ready?" I smiled, trying to hide the tear that threatened to fall and ruin my carefully applied makeup. Deep down, I couldn't shake off the feeling that this decision wasn't quite right or perhaps not the right time. I knew in my heart that I would have to fight to make this marriage work. But I pushed those doubts aside and nodded confidently at my dad.

I overlooked the issue of pornography until Nate was exposed again less than a year into our marriage. I quickly realized that what I'd thought was a good marriage wasn't as strong as I had believed—more lies stood between us. With no money to our name, we relied heavily on my extern nurse position at Methodist Hospital, where I earned fifteen dollars per hour, to cover our monthly bills. It was a decent amount back then, but the program only offered twenty hours a week.

Nate was working at the Omni Hotel as a concierge, but his tips were unpredictable and often insufficient to meet ends. Every month, we faced the same struggle: juggling bills and expenses, hoping we wouldn't overdraft and be hit with a twenty-five-dollar charge for each overdraft. By the end of the month, we were usually left with a negative balance of two hundred dollars.

I could see the strain taking its toll on Nate as he managed our finances. He became overwhelmed at times and would withdraw. We desperately needed some help and intervention, but we didn't know where to start, and we were both trying so hard. We continued on this path, both too proud to admit to anyone we needed help.

One night, Nate asked me if he could watch a game with a few of his buddies from work. I had no reason to question his plans until he stayed out into the early hours of the night. Despite his reassurances that there was nothing to worry about, something didn't quite add up since he was getting home well past the time that the game had finished. This happened on a number of occasions.

Adding to my concern, Nate would become visibly upset whenever I inquired about his whereabouts or probed into the details. The situation left me with unease and a growing need for clarification. I knew something wasn't right, yet I desperately wanted to believe that he had no intention to harm or hurt me—so I believed him. Finances continued to be a source of frustration, as our bills would frequently accumulate, leaving us in the red. Yet, here we were, living in downtown Dallas trying our best to figure out married life.

As graduation approached and the responsibilities of adulthood drew near, Nate and I felt a strong pull to return to the Valley in south Texas. My parents worked hard building a medical clinic ministry in Nuevo Progreso, just over the border in Mexico, and we felt called to help. During this time, I was also offered an impressive new job as a registered nurse in the operating room of a hospital near my parents (the salary was $65,000 per year, with an additional $10,000 bonus, an amount that seemed like a fortune to me). We were excited to move. The weight of this decision sat heavily on our shoulders, but we both knew deep down that it was the right path for us.

CLINIC GROWING

My parents organized volunteer groups from various states in the United States and constructed a two-story, 6,000 square-foot concrete building that encompassed the Bible school in Nuevo Progreso. The clinic featured several bathrooms, a complete septic system, and running water, which was a desired commodity in that area. A large room upstairs housed two dental chairs, an X-ray machine, multiple rooms with examination tables and every medical supply needed, and an impressively extensive pharmacy that could rival many. The clinic also offered an ophthalmology exam room. Typically, around twenty individuals, including doctors, nurses, nurse practitioners, translators, and volunteers conducted these monthly clinics, during which they would see around two hundred people. With the help of many, the clinic ran smoothly and was quite productive medically.

My parents, although Dad would modestly say that Mom ran the clinic, worked together so well. They also traveled further into the interior of Mexico, engaging in building projects. Sometimes they built an entire home or a church in as little as a week, while some projects included adding a septic system, running water, and electricity.

What made the clinic truly special was its focus on ministering to each person who walked through the doors. Mom would emphasize that their real purpose was not just to offer medication or a Band-Aid; it was to introduce people to Jesus—the ultimate source of healing. "People are more open when they are shown kindness and concern, which opens doors of opportunity to speak to their spiritual needs."

My parents accomplished truly remarkable feats because their focus was to follow the command of Jesus: to love God and love people. They weren't trying to accumulate an abundance of wealth or make a name for themselves; instead, everything they needed seemed to be miraculously provided.

Though my parents were successfully running the clinic, Nate and I, however, held concerns about Mom's and Dad's health and age. In our eyes, they were getting up there in years, and we questioned how long they could manage all these responsibilities. Little did we fully comprehend all that God was doing. My parents never experienced age as a hindrance, and because they were called to this ministry, the Lord granted them the necessary grace to fulfill their work.

With concerns in mind, Nate and I packed our apartment and made our way back to live in the Valley of South Texas. When we arrived, intending to "help" Mom and Dad, we soon observed they were doing just fine and really didn't need our help, but they were always grateful to have us around. We also discovered that they had become well-known in Nuevo Progreso, earning favor not only with the Mexican people and government but also with their counterparts in the United States. Witnessing the unity of the body of Christ coming together to serve others was truly a beautiful experience. As we began helping with the clinics, we saw individuals working together as a team and relying on one another. Each volunteer played a critical part—the doctors, workers, prayer warriors, and translators.

Dad would often talk about the profound impact that crossing a bridge could have. A simple bridge, connecting two countries, could take you into an entirely different world. I have a vivid memory of a specific occasion when I crossed the bridge into Nuevo Progreso, Mexico, with my mom. As we walked down the streets, thirty people or more enthusiastically called out her name, "Hoody, Hoody," meaning Judi in Spanish. Some approached her seeking assistance, while others came with smiles and hugs. Regardless of their requests, Mom always made a point to show each person love in her unique way.

I was in awe of my mom's love, not just for me but for what felt like all the people of Mexico. Despite the fact that these people had nothing to offer her, she embraced each person with love in her eyes and her heart. While processing all of this, I was still trying to understand my own prejudices. At some point during those years of volunteering and helping in the clinic, I experienced a transformation in my own life. That's when I realized, "Wow, my situation isn't as bad as I thought; I could have been the one living in these circumstances." In a surreal moment, my entire life seemed to play out before me in slow motion. Memories of my parents serving others with compassion and dedication flooded my mind. I could see them as they labored to clean toilets and floors and dig trenches or mix concrete on the ground. Their selflessness and love were evident in every action, all with the purpose of improving other people's lives and leading them toward Jesus.

I watched in awe as my mother embraced individuals with various ailments and diseases, not afraid of their illness, her arms wrapping around them with genuine love and compassion. It was a sight that had become all too familiar to me, since, for all of my life, I had been the one receiving such care and attention during countless surgeries.

I remember a time when my mom gave away her shoes, walked home barefoot, and despite not having much, she responded, "They're just shoes. I can get more." This pattern continued with her necklace and clothing. Mom put aside her own needs so she could help those around her. Her hospitality and love knew no bounds.

My dad's example of serving others was just like my mom's. Yes, he was a teacher and preacher, but he worked physically whenever he saw a need, whether it meant digging a ditch or trench, or working an extra job to help support others. He worked tirelessly, but his real strength was his humility. He is the humblest man I have ever known.

He set his own achievements aside and highlighted the accomplishments of others to empower them for the greater good of the body of Christ. Despite facing adversity and being mistreated by others, he harbors no need to be proven right. He just silently continues to move forward, following wherever Jesus leads.

Thankfully, something finally shifted within me as I witnessed my parents' selfless acts of kindness, and I finally understood the importance of loving and serving others. My heart shifted from wanting to be served to serving and seeing others as a priority.

In this community of sick and hurting people, I felt no need for defenses or to prove anything. I already knew I was loved, and now, something inside of me wanted to love others in return. People began to see me as someone willing to lend a helping hand and assist. I had no problem getting in the grossest places and cleaning, where previously I would have been repelled. I was now learning it wasn't about me. I transitioned from imitating my parents' actions of service to a change in my heart, where my efforts of trying to "do my duty" became a natural part of who I wanted to be.

By learning to love others, the chains of prejudice that once bound me began to melt away. I began to look for the content of a person's character rather than just seeing the color of their skin. That is also when I began to appreciate and accept my own uniqueness and realized that no race or person is inferior to another.

I began to be proud of my heritage. I observed its culture, its love for family and community, and its dedication to hard work despite having received little in return. The Bible says that God created us all in His image; therefore, we are handcrafted, set apart, and made to make our mark differently than someone else. I was no longer ashamed of who I was, but I was proud that I was born in Guatemala, and my biological parents had made it possible for me to live in freedom.

My parents' initial expectations of serving in the interior of Mexico didn't align with where they were currently living in the Valley. Back in 1997, the air hung heavy with grief as my dad stood alone in the Washington State cemetery where his mother was laid to rest. In the quiet solitude of that moment, surrounded by the weight of his loss, he heard the Lord's voice—with a clarity that surpassed any previous encounter. The words echoed, "I told you to move to the Valley, but I haven't told you to leave." This pivotal moment became a directive that reshaped the course of our family's future, leading us to settle permanently in the Rio Grande Valley.

God unfolded a much larger plan, surpassing any vision we could have conceived. If we had moved to the interior of Mexico when we first arrived in the Rio Grande Valley, I would not have the correct papers and probably would not have been able to obtain my citizenship, which would have prevented my remaining in the States.

However, God in His providence protected us. Thankfully, Dad listened to the voice of God and was obedient. My parents were able to work on the border and establish an amazing ministry, called Cornerstone Ministry, that impacted several nations. Their work turned out to be greater than what they could have initially imagined.

Unfortunately, years later in 2010, the Mexican cartel's influence was on the rise and numerous threats loomed over the clinic. In Nuevo Progreso, Mexico, most vendors had succumbed to paying fees to the cartel in order to stay in business. The most alarming development was the increasing reports of kidnappings, and it seemed as though my parents had become potential targets. The security level warning escalated from yellow to red, leading to the closure of the bridge at times, and they were strongly advised not to return to the clinic for their safety.

This situation was heartbreaking. They had poured years of sweat equity and tears into the ministry of the clinic, and I believe a part of their hearts remains embedded with the Mexican people. Yet, despite the turmoil taking place in the region, God was working in ways yet unknown to us.

MARRIAGE: CHANGE, CHAINS, AND CYCLES OF BONDAGE

During the earlier times of the clinic's success, I started my dream job as a registered nurse in an operating room. I wanted to know what it was like to be on the other side during surgery. Meanwhile, Nate graduated with a double major in psychology and sociology with a minor in biblical studies and was a self-taught computer genius. We still contributed our efforts to the clinic whenever time allowed. Nate's job search was off to a rough start as he faced the stark reality that an undergraduate psychology degree didn't offer abundant opportunities and he didn't speak Spanish, which was a requirement for many of the jobs in the Rio Grande Valley.

Simultaneously, as he and I worked together to build the foundation of our new lives, a sense of unease hung in the air. Communication with Nate was difficult, and I struggled to set boundaries or express my needs, which left me feeling frustrated and resentful. I struggled to find a way to be assertive without coming across as rude or abrupt. Despite the image of a seemingly "perfect" marriage outside our home, issues with pornography, dishonesty, and outbursts of anger on both our parts were constantly lurking and threatened to tear apart the delicate balance we had managed to maintain behind closed doors. Little did I know, things were about to take a turn for the worse.

CHAPTER FOURTEEN

Warfare

For two years, I rotated between various operating rooms specialties, but my main surgical room was the children's dental room. In that environment, I collaborated closely with the hospital owner, who was an anesthesiologist—a quiet and introspective man whom I was determined to befriend. Because we saw eye to eye on most topics, we worked extremely well together. However, after years of working in the OR, I began to yearn for new challenges and a change of scenery.

The recovery room nurses were known to have some of the most challenging roles in our hospital, and I wanted to be a part of it. I expressed my desire to explore different areas within the hospital. As I approached the director's office to request a move to the recovery room, my heart raced. The director herself was a commanding presence, exuding confidence that made me feel both intimidated and intrigued. With striking features and an unyielding gaze, she was not someone to be trifled with. After hearing my request, she suggested starting in the women's recovery room, which had just been built and offered a slower learning pace, seeing only about twenty cases a day compared to the main hospital that was seeing close to sixty-five cases a day. Despite the warning signs that the recovery room would be filled with predominantly type A nurses, known for their high energy and competitiveness, I couldn't resist the opportunity to learn and grow in such an environment. I was determined to put in the hard work necessary for a successful transition.

Transitioning from the operating room to the recovery room, I faced two significant challenges that tested my skills and resilience. First, in the recovery room, unlike the structured environment of the operating room where the anesthesiologist oversees most patient care, each patient was directly under my responsibility. This demanded an enhancement of my critical thinking skills, which had lain dormant for years while I'd worked in the operating room. One crucial skill I had to quickly master was the delicate task of extubating patients, which means carefully removing the endotracheal tube post-surgery. Second, I found myself in an unhealthy work environment with a group of colleagues who resembled high school mean girls rather than seasoned medical professionals. Gossip, hatred, and envy were commonplace, creating a toxic atmosphere. Despite these obstacles, I remained determined to excel in my new role and prove myself despite their unprofessional behavior.

Confident and well-liked by doctors and anesthesiologists, I would openly share about my personal life and journey of overcoming challenges, though the nurses in the recovery room weren't receptive to my stories. It was then I learned that sometimes blending in, not standing out or speaking up, is the better approach to fitting in. Despite warnings I experienced in the unit, I chose to stay, determined to succeed and make the best of the situation.

I was often assigned the most complex patients with minimal information offered during report, and so I faced public chastisement from fellow nurses in front of patients. Unfounded accusations were sometimes made, creating an environment where my voice felt gradually suppressed. Colleagues seemed to hope for my failure, actively pushing me out, reminiscent again of my high school years. I found it challenging to be around individuals who sought to gain the upper hand by questioning me to gauge my knowledge. They seemed ready to strike like a snake on every failure I made. I tried to meet them with kindness and compassion, but I found myself trying to make it work only for their approval. In truth, I was not a saint in this situation. I became annoyed because my kindness was not being reciprocated, which led to feelings of resentment.

As a last resort, which perhaps should have been my first, I mustered up the courage to stand up for myself and voice my preferences and speak up. This taught me that I desperately needed to learn the balance between being a peacemaker and being assertive toward injustices. However, my decision to speak up came with unforeseen consequences.

During this time, Nate and I were trying for our first child and we were thrilled to learn I was pregnant. In our excitement we told all of our family and friends. One weekend I was called in for a case weeks into my pregnancy. I was alone on the unit with the anesthesiologist just a call away. My patient, just out of surgery, seemed stable and responded to my question, "Can you squeeze my hand?"

but as I began removing the endotracheal tube, her body tensed up and she started experiencing laryngeal spasms. With the tube out, I saw her oxygen saturation levels declining. I began puffing oxygen manually because she was not breathing on her own, and under my breath, I said a quick prayer, "Lord!"

My patient coughed a few times, which fortunately resolved the issue. Her oxygen levels began to rise and went up to 99 percent on room air without the use of oxygen. She was stabilized, and as a sigh of relief crossed my face suddenly, it felt as though I'd been punched in the gut. I bent over, gasping for breath. Somehow, I stayed with the patient and had the front desk call to transport the patient to her room; while I stepped away running to the bathroom, I discovered a personal tragedy—I was having a miscarriage. During the pain of Nate's and my loss, hurtful rumors began to spread about my pregnancy and miscarriage being fabricated as an excuse to avoid work. It was a painful reminder of how judgmental and callous people could be.

It was a very difficult time, but God was there working behind the scenes. He was ready to rescue me from the rejection, always providing redirection. Shortly after my miscarriage, I was called to human resources early in the morning by my stern head supervisor, who was not always approachable. As I left the recovery room, I could tell the nurses knew something I didn't. Without warning, I was informed by human resources that I would be transferred to a different area in the hospital. They collected my badges and scrubs, leaving me utterly blindsided. I later discovered that a couple of coworkers had accused me of things that were simply untrue.

While my sense of justice urged me to set things straight, I realized I couldn't prove anything—and I really had nothing to prove. I was given options, but most involved a significant pay decrease. There were a couple of open areas, one in labor and delivery. One open spot in the behavioral psychiatric unit would allow me to retain my current pay rate, but I could only work PRN (from the Latin pro re nata, as needed).

At that time, I had no understanding of what it would be like to work in the behavioral psychiatric unit. However, since my childhood, I'd harbored a dream of someday working in prisons, and I perceived that this position would be somewhat similar. Besides, my main focus at the time was to ensure my professional survival. I found myself questioning why this was happening and why certain individuals seemed to harbor a dislike toward me. Throughout my life, a recurring pattern emerged, particularly since high school: girls rejected me and made me feel unwanted. This raised doubts in my mind about whether I might be the problem.

PSYCH UNIT

Transitioning to the psychiatric unit initially felt intimidating. I was issued a badge that granted me access in and out of the building and certain rooms, and some rooms were completely secluded and had padded walls. This unit comprised four sections: the children's unit, adolescent unit, adult unit, and geriatric unit. At first glance, I only saw about one guard to every four to six patients on each unit. I relaxed when I realized the guards were actually staff technicians who had a great camaraderie. They were friendly, happy, laughing, making jokes, and genuinely enjoyed the time they worked together. Notably, I observed a mix of both men and women, which was a welcomed difference.

Immersing myself in my new job, I soon realized that I possessed more knowledge than some of the staff when it came to nursing skills. Some of them had been in the unit for an extended period and had lost certain skills, particularly in tasks like starting IVs, especially with pediatric patients, a skill I had mastered in the operating room. It felt like I had moved from a valley to the mountaintop in just a day.

My responsibilities varied as I rotated through each unit, taking on roles such as charge nurse, floor nurse attending to patients, or handling medications. Each area had its advantages and disadvantages. I particularly enjoyed the times when I engaged with patients on the floor, learning their unique stories during the admission process. This involved approximately thirty minutes of one-on-one time to gain insights into their backgrounds.

Working in the psychiatric unit felt like a breath of fresh air, prompting me to wonder why I hadn't made the move sooner. I was finally working with supportive colleagues that encouraged and helped me when needed. Nate and I were also trying again for another baby, and a year later, we became pregnant with a boy.

While life and work were great, I came into contact with the supernatural. I knew about the supernatural realm as a little girl; however, as I grew it was as if it were a distant memory. On Halloween eve the unit was at maximum capacity, and as I stepped through the locked doors of the unit, I felt something shift. It felt as if two protective, powerful beings were walking alongside me, giving me a sense that angels were present for my protection.

I navigated through the locked doors, only to be greeted by a room filled with unpredictable patients exhibiting unusual behavior. Among them, a woman stood out, twirling around like a fairy on an adrenaline rush. Amid the chaos, her intense gaze fixated on me, and she followed my every move.

The situation escalated when she jumped onto a chair, undressed, and stood entirely naked, never breaking eye contact. Her twirling finger seemed ominous. Feeling a surge of fear, especially now being pregnant with Ethan, I instinctively placed my hand on my stomach and asked for the blood of Jesus to cover me.

In that moment, I felt a warming sensation descending from the top of my head to the soles of my feet. The warmth intensified until my feet felt extremely hot. Uncertain of what was happening, I wondered if it was related to my B vitamins or perhaps something worse. The medication nurse administered a sedative cocktail of Haldol and Ativan, an antipsychotic combination, which calmed her down. Thankfully, the floor techs intervened and gently managed the situation, covering the naked patient. The woman continued to be unpredictable for the remainder of the shift but presented no harm to herself or anyone else, including me.

Returning home that evening, I shared the experience with Nate, expressing concern that the woman may have cast a spell on me. Nathan, however, interrupted and asked about my prayer. I explained that I had prayed for the blood of Jesus to cover me. He clarified that what I felt was the power of the Holy Spirit, the protective cover of the blood of Jesus. Instantly, a sense of peace washed over me, reassuring me that the Holy Spirit had shielded me that day.

SPIRITUAL WARFARE

Our staff was comprised of individuals from diverse backgrounds and beliefs, including Catholics, Christians, atheists, agnostics, Hindus, and Jews. Others knew I was a follower of Jesus Christ, and I maintained mutual respect with my colleagues. I stood firm in my beliefs with genuine love and respect for others, without compromising my personal convictions, and I received the same respect.

Every day in the unit, I witnessed the intersection of the physical and spiritual realms. Maybe that explains why, one particular evening, while sleeping at home, I had an exceptionally vivid dream. I discovered that I had been transported to a dimly lit wooden attic and was positioned near the top of an A-frame structure with high ceilings near a window.

When I looked down, I saw myself sitting on one side of a bench, and a lady with curly dark hair sat across from me. Initially, our conversation was cordial, but as it progressed, it took a more intense turn. We both stood up and leaned toward each other in what appeared to be a heated argument. I witnessed red, swirling fire coming from her mouth, met by blue fiery material with musical notes clashing with the flames. I could see anger in her eyes, and then the dream abruptly ended. I woke up, sat upright in bed, took a deep breath, and checked my body to ensure I was no longer dreaming.

I attempted to go back to sleep, but an overwhelming sense of fear covered me as if there were someone else in the room, someone invisible. I sought refuge under the covers briefly, and then mustered the courage to wake Nate.

Nate was visibly startled, having been in a deep sleep. He asked if I was okay, and I shared that I had a nightmare, and requested him to pray for me. Nate began to pray, rebuking any curses or hexes that might have been spoken over me. Remarkably, as he continued to pray, it felt as though a weight had been lifted, and the paralyzing fear I had felt just moments before dissipated. I was then able to go back to sleep.

The following morning, I expressed my gratitude for his prayer over me and shared how specific his prayer had been. However, when I mentioned the content of his prayer, he seemed surprised and said, "I don't remember praying for you."

Upon entering work the next morning, everything seemed normal. I was assigned to be the floor nurse in the adult unit, and the room was exceptionally crowded. People were scattered everywhere, sitting on the floor against the walls and in chairs. The night shift staff had stayed overtime to assist in taking vital signs from the patients, supporting the day shift.

As I scanned the room, my attention was drawn to a lady who was sitting quietly in a chair while her blood pressure was being measured. I squinted and looked closer when all the blood seemed to drain from my body. I held my breath and was momentarily frozen in place. If you thought I had seen a ghost, you wouldn't have been far off. It was the lady from my dream the previous night. I noticed her first, but as I stood there, paralyzed by fear, she also noticed me and did a double take. When our eyes met, it was as if we both recognized each other from my dream.

I wasn't sure how to react. Should I keep my distance and ignore her? Or should I try to approach her and get to know her? Questions swirled in my mind.

I avoided her for the first thirty minutes, but then I remembered that fear is not of the Lord, and I couldn't avoid her for the next twelve hours I was on duty. I quickly ran to the nurse's unit, looked up her file and skimmed through all the information about what had brought her to the hospital. I even asked coworkers about her. After a deep breath, I engaged in small talk with her as I jotted down her blood pressure. While recording her vitals, I was drawn to her many satanic tattoos. Her tattoos validated the accuracy of my dream. She was pleasant when speaking, but she also noticed my gaze shift toward her tattoos. I hate to admit it, but I was afraid to be alone around her. So, I sought refuge in the medication room with a male nurse I trusted named Joe. I also knew the half door was locked, so the chances of her confronting me there were lower than in the open day room. I did ask my colleagues to keep a close eye on me, and they agreed. However, I didn't share all the details of my dream with them, or else they might have admitted me as a patient that day.

When this patient approached the medication room door, she stood behind another patient and made clicking sounds with her mouth. The clicks started off slowly and then gradually sped up. I was left stunned, unsure how to respond. As she got closer to the door, she said, "I can feel the energy." Without any prompting from me, she began to share the story of what had led her to the psych unit.

She told me about her encounter with a few Christians the previous night. As they prayed for her, she claimed that she started climbing the walls in an unnatural manner and her head twisted around, reminiscent of a scene from The Exorcist. I couldn't verify the truth of her story, but considering my dream, it didn't seem impossible. I didn't know what to say or how to respond so I quickly handed her the scheduled medication. She remarked that I have a lot of light in me, to which I simply replied, "Thank you." Then, she simply walked away to the day room, and I never saw her again after my shift was over.

This experience marked the beginning of my eyes being opened to the spiritual world that exists. Later, as I reflected on the situation, I questioned whether I could have done more to share the love of Jesus with her. I wondered about the purpose of my dream. However, I believe that the Lord allowed me a glimpse into the spiritual realm to prepare me in advance for what I needed to identify and then prepare spiritually in prayer. Yes, I prayed for spiritual covering, but I know now I had nothing to fear, only something to share.

A GHOST IN THE UNIT

I remember a specific day when David, a floor staff member whom I greatly admired and considered a friend, discovered my interest in the supernatural and the spiritual realm. Having shared some of my experiences with him, he proceeded to tell me about a ghost that had reportedly been seen in our unit earlier that week. Although intrigued, I wasn't entirely sure if I believed in ghosts, and I must admit, the idea scared me a bit.

David, along with another coworker, urged me to visit room five, claiming they had encountered a ghost there. Initially, I thought it was all a joke, but when they insisted and even mentioned a picture, they had my attention. David showed me a picture on his cell phone featuring a blurry figure in the corner of the room. I was astonished; they had captured a ghost in a photograph.

They encouraged me to do some supernatural warfare. I felt a mix of terror and curiosity as I approached room five. I set my alarm, for a quick escape, took a deep breath, prayed silently, and slowly entered the room. Much to my surprise, there was no floating girl in the corner. David explained that she must have left when she sensed my arrival.

I requested to see the photo again, and after a couple of days of banter, David confessed it had all been a joke. They had fabricated the "ghost" by cutting out a spooky girl from a magazine cover, attaching her to a popsicle stick, and then taking a picture with her in the room. I was genuinely amazed at their creativity. They got me—we all shared a good laugh. You know you're truly "in" with others when they feel comfortable enough to prank you. They knew me enough to know I could take a prank. Finally reaching that level, I felt a sense of belonging and acceptance that I hadn't experienced working in other units.

DANGEROUS TERRITORY

In my third trimester of pregnancy, exhaustion set in from working twelve-hour shifts, sometimes four to five days a week. Nate surprised me one day by suggesting a lunch date the next day since I was off from work. Excited, I headed to his office the next afternoon, even though I couldn't reach him over the phone. After multiple attempts, he finally answered, speaking in a whisper. Curious about our lunch plans, I asked where he was and why he was whispering.

My heart dropped when he revealed he was with a female colleague, Amber, helping her with a printer issue at her house. A surge of panic and betrayal rippled through me as he sheepishly explained that he had lost track of time and forgot to call me.

Several concerns weighed on my mind. First, Nate never informed me he was going to her house. Second, he had never made house calls before then. So, I was guessing this wasn't work-related. The lack of communication raised questions about transparency and inclusion. To add to my unease, Nate had previously expressed to me that he found Amber to be stunningly beautiful. Devastated, I hung up the phone, overwhelmed by a sense of hopelessness and a whirlwind of emotions—anger, sadness, and hurt. When we saw each other at home, my emotions erupted, and Nate matched my intensity, attempting to control the situation. He grabbed my arms as I tried to walk away, wanting to avoid him after we'd had a yelling match. I needed more time to process my feelings and question the facts since nothing added up. Nate, quick and articulate with words, skillfully redirected the conversation toward me, leaving me feeling cornered. I was still learning how to be assertive, thus in response, became physical, pushing him away and resorting to hitting or throwing objects to create distance.

    Nate gave me a grand story, stating that Amber's nanny was at the house. However, later, Nate said that Amber's husband and children were there, not her nanny, as he had initially claimed. Nate denied ever saying that Amber's nanny was at the house and said I misunderstood or did not hear correctly. The story changed several times. Though he said I could call Amber or her husband to verify his story, I couldn't bring myself to call. Later, Nate told me he spoke with Amber and asked if I could speak with her husband, but she requested that I not involve her husband to avoid causing issues in her marriage. I felt a sense of shame, torn between not believing Nate's story and wrongly accusing Amber. I was entertaining the possibility that there might be more to the situation, but I had no evidence to prove my case.

COUNSELOR

Amid our ongoing arguments regarding Amber and a brief separation, Nate stayed at my parents' house, and we reluctantly concluded that seeking a counselor was necessary. Nate also agreed to undergo a polygraph test, specifically regarding both pornography and Amber, that I demanded he do if we were going to stay together. Unsure about where to turn, we chose the only counselor we'd heard about at our church, highly recommended by fellow members.

    Nate, well-prepared, entered the counselor's office with a manila envelope containing meticulously highlighted and dated copies of our text conversations. This orchestrated setup became apparent as he had stopped texting a month ago, responding only with brief answers while I continued sending novels.

I walked into the counselor's office unprepared to present my side, confident that the situation was straightforward and that I had already won. It didn't occur to me that the counselor might disagree with me. So, when the counselor turned to me, I struggled to articulate my concerns about Nate's pornography, lying, and interactions with Amber. I could not remember the exact wording from our arguments nor the exact incidents that left the counselor looking at me perplexed. As I finished, the focus shifted to Nate, who eloquently admitted his involvement in pornography and took ownership of his part. However, he insisted that I should also own my part, listing detailed instances where I had thrown things at him, hit him, and yelled. However, he conveniently left out what had pushed me to that point or his own similar behavior toward me. At that moment, I couldn't perceive any faults in myself, nor did I have the inclination to acknowledge any, as I firmly believed I was in the right and he was in the wrong. In retrospect, I recognize that I was adopting an arrogant stance of self-righteousness.

The counselor's expressions indicated support for Nate, nodding and shaking his head. The session veered away from the core issue I'd intended to address, placing the spotlight solely on me. The counselor said I might be an overbearing wife, prone to overreacting, and speculated that my heated tantrums were contributing to Nate's pornography problem. I sensed a certain satisfaction on

Nate's face as if he relished the counselor's rebuke of me. It seemed like he and the counselor were sharing a moment of camaraderie. Nate had told me numerous times that I needed to be "corrected," and this counselor seemed to fulfill that role. Outnumbered, I wanted to scream and escape the office, but I sat there and took the blame, being labeled as the problem in our relationship. To add to it, the counselor diagnosed me with anxiety, which, at the time, I thought he was wrong about. I also felt like he was just slapping this word on me without understanding the entirety of our situation.

From that moment on, the idea of stepping into a counselor's office terrified me. Trust seemed shattered, and the only people I felt safe around were my parents. However, my parents, because they are amazing, stayed neutral. The weight of my husband's betrayal overwhelmed me as if I had endured two heavy blows that threatened to knock me down. I found myself at a loss for words and unsure of how to convey my emotions or navigate the situation. Neither of us were prepared to take personal responsibility; instead, we persisted in blaming each other.

Nate did go through with the polygraph test. However, the polygraph examiner couldn't comprehend why we would spend money on such a test, asserting it's a common behavior for every guy to be involved in pornography, even stating his involvement. However, he lacked the knowledge of our personal story, the years of deception, lies, cover-ups, betrayal, and addiction. The examiner asked me to leave while he performed the test. Despite the polygraph results coming back as passing, indicating honesty, all of us were acutely aware that it didn't reflect the heart of the truth.

THERAPIST SESSIONS

On my way to the psychiatric behavioral unit at 5:30 a.m., driving my dad's old blue pickup truck, I was overwhelmed and crying out to God in desperation. Tears relentlessly streamed down my face as I begged God to change me, to transform my heart. Deep down, I knew something wasn't right within me. I even feared the worst, entertaining thoughts of having an undiagnosed psychiatric disorder. Between the ongoing tension with Nate, the loss of friendships in my life, and feeling hostility from those around me, I pleaded, "God, I need you—I need you; I don't know what is going on with me, but, Lord, I am not right. God, I am begging you to take my life and to remove anything in my life that isn't right and make me whole again." I sat in the truck, pouring out my heart to the Lord until I had no more tears left to cry.

On that particular day at work, I found myself on the unit floor, accompanying patients to their classes and the lunchroom. Ana Delia was filling in for the main therapist, who was off for the week. Ana Delia, a beautiful Spanish woman with dark, flowing black hair, displayed a warm and caring demeanor as she connected with each patient in our semicircle, and looked deeply into each person's eyes. She then pulled out what looked like a child's book. The whole room had confused expressions as she began reading The Tale of Three Trees, a folktale about the aspirations of three trees. The first tree becomes beautiful, the second grows strong, and the third aspires to be the tallest. After being forgotten in a woodpile, the third tree doesn't achieve its height goal. However, it discovers a greater purpose as the cross that holds Jesus. Now, every time people see this tree, they think of Jesus, which was more meaningful than simply being the tallest.

Though I held back outward emotions, I was left with a stiff neck and sore throat in the process, as it touched me right at the core of my being, just as I was starting to lose sight of my dreams and plans. It served as a gentle reminder of how important I am to God and encouraged me to trust in His plan, which was to point others to Him.

That week, I requested to be part of the floor staff so I could attend each one of Ana Delia's groups. Each time she spoke, it felt as though she was addressing me directly, and I found myself on the verge of tears. I left each session feeling changed. After spending the entire week in Ana Delia's groups, which were free counseling sessions, I mustered the courage to ask if I could see her individually. I feared that it might be crossing a work relationship boundary, but to my surprise, she eagerly agreed.

During our one-on-one sessions, tears freely flowed as we discussed various topics, including adoption, rejection, Nate, codependency, trauma, and my need for self-protection. I shared with her my realization that I was witnessing a self-fulfilling prophecy unfolding in every aspect of my life. My preconceptions and expectations were shaping my outcomes. For instance, anticipating that a person would eventually not like me led me to keep them at arm's length. Consequently, when they did express disapproval later on, it reinforced this pattern. I was gripped by fear of rejection, which resulted in me rejecting others before they had a chance to reject me. This introspection led me to question whether I might be the root cause of many of my challenges. Despite my fear of the truth, I craved clarity, sensing a growing bitterness within me and a diminishing joy.

Toward the end of our sessions, I finally gathered the courage to ask Ana Delia about my anxiety diagnosis. I wrestled with the fear of even more potential diagnoses, as Nate was concerned there was something seriously wrong with me. Her reassuring response, accompanied by a smile, was, "Camey, yes, you have anxiety, but do you know what the opposite of anxiety is?" I looked at her without any response, as though I was flipping through my mental Rolodex to come up with the best answer I could muster. Before I could give my best guess, she said, "The opposite of anxiety is 'trust.'" With a gentle smile, she asked if I was able to trust Nate. "No," she said, "because he hasn't shown you anything to prove his trustworthiness. Are you able to trust others?"

The only people I knew I could trust were my parents, family, and doctors. Yet, I hadn't seriously thought about the ones I couldn't trust. She asked, "Do you trust yourself?" and then, lastly, she inquired, "Do you trust God?" She went on to explain that anxiety is sometimes rooted in fear—the fear of facing challenges alone or the fear of feeling unsafe, which can lead to codependency. On the other hand, trust is built on knowledge of the truth, accountability, safety, and honesty. She continued, "Camey, you must learn to trust God in everything because His plan is the best for you. He is for you and not against you. From what you've shared with me, you've seen His faithfulness in your life time and time again. You must come to a point where you can trust yourself again. You are smart, and I am fully confident that you can and will make the right decisions. God has equipped you with everything you need to fulfill your assignment here on Earth."

I sat there, taking every word to heart, yet unable to fully process everything she was saying. I was taking notes and was truly determined to have a better understanding of myself and all she had shared with me. Before my session ended, I inquired about medication or any special prescription that I needed, to which she replied with another heartfelt smile, "Nope, you don't need anything. Everything you've experienced and how you've responded aligns." I took a deep breath and let out a sigh of weighted relief, realizing I wasn't as unstable as I had come to believe. However, I knew I needed to do some more interpersonal work.

THE COUNTERFEIT

During my five years in the behavioral psychiatric unit, I learned valuable lessons. I discovered the importance of doing my best at work while also embracing a lighthearted approach, not taking myself or those around me too seriously. Laughter became a powerful tool in building connections and understanding one another.

Although I never personally experienced admission to the psychiatric unit, the realization that we are all just one step away from such an experience became evident. I saw patients who were doctors, lawyers, known musicians, famous actors, pilots, millionaires, homeless individuals, Christians, and non-Christians—people from all different walks of life. I wasn't able to hear each unique story or discover the reasons behind their actions, the "why" that caused them to respond in a certain way to the world around them.

But I grew in my knowledge about human behavior, understanding that every person fights battles against hurts, fears, rejections, insecurities, and hidden wounds that others know nothing about or will never understand.

Some people ended up in the unit against their will, while others were there due to their own destructive choices, struggles with addiction, family issues, mental health challenges, or chemical imbalances. No matter the cause, we all face moments of turmoil that none of us are immune to. While I did not perform exorcisms, I did learn about spiritual warfare and how to discern different spirits. I learned that even demons liked the medication. One patient even told me, "I need my meds now or my demon will show itself." This was no veiled threat. Some patients unintentionally opened themselves up to demonic influences through games and activities, not realizing the potential consequences. The enemy truly seeks to steal, kill and destroy by spreading lies and encouraging self-harm. I saw people slither on the floor like snakes, witnessed children scale walls with unnatural strength, and heard man-like voices that didn't align with small children's voices. Each experience equipped me with a deeper knowledge of the spiritual realm. Yes, I was afraid at times, but most of the time I was more curious than fearful. I sought to see the invisible chains that held people captive, and desired to gain an understanding so I could point them toward the One who could set them free.

The very place where I was rejected became the door to redirection. As a little girl, I had attended a healing conference in New Orleans and witnessed the manifestation of God's power. Now, at the behavioral psychiatric hospital, I observed the power of the enemy—the counterfeit that harms rather than heals.

SPARED

Because of my calling, the enemy has relentlessly tried to take me out since before I even took my first breath. Once, I experienced a T-bone collision in a hit-and-run situation when the other driver recklessly ran through a red light, causing my car to spin as I gripped the steering wheel tightly.

I witnessed the other driver fleeing the scene. Miraculously, I emerged from the incident without a scratch, and a compassionate bystander took it upon himself to chase down the other driver. Fortunately, the responsible party was apprehended and covered all the necessary car repairs.

In another incident, I nearly drowned. For about thirty minutes, I was bobbing up and down over the waves, reaching a point where I could no longer touch the ground after being pushed farther out into the ocean.

The power of the ocean proved relentless, repeatedly dragging me under with each wave. My lungs burned for air as I struggled to keep my head above the water. Six brave individuals swam to my rescue, although only two managed to reach me. Each grabbed an arm, inadvertently making me feel like they were pushing me under even more.

Just as I felt on the verge of drowning, a man on a surfboard reached me and brought me back to shore. The six swimmers collapsed on the sand, gasping for breath, and recovered with an ambulance administering oxygen. Meanwhile, I stood there, feeling a mix of embarrassment and immense gratitude toward each person who tried to rescue me. I wanted to express my thanks to the man on the surfboard, but he was nowhere in sight.

I also encountered a head injury during my college years when the sharp edge of a car door slammed into the back of my head due to a strong gust of wind. It sent a searing pain through my skull, resulting in a permanent dent that also exacerbated my forgetfulness. For a few minutes, everything went black, and I was left off-balance, diagnosed with a concussion.

Then another terrifying incident unfolded when the brakes on my Mazda Miata failed, and I let out an ear-piercing scream. I careened down an icy hill, with a red traffic light looming in front of me. My heart pounded in my chest, as I realized I had lost control of my car. Desperately, I tried to navigate through oncoming traffic, narrowly avoiding a potentially catastrophic collision.

All of these potential death experiences remind me that Psalms 139:16 says that God has numbered our days even before we were born, so He alone knows when we will breathe our last breath here on Earth. God is still writing my story—for my good and His glory.

CHAPTER FIFTEEN

On or Off Stage

Upon a recommendation from some friends, Nate and I entered a vast, stylish, bustling building. Our customary preference was to head to the balcony where we would remain unnoticed. However, as we sat listening to a group of singers holding microphones, the sound stirred our emotions and brought tears to our eyes. Soon after the music concluded, a tall, handsome, and charismatic speaker took the stage, reminiscent of the pastors we knew in Dallas. He commanded the attention of the audience with his presence, and we hung onto his every word. Nate and I exchanged glances, silently knowing that this would become our home church.

We faithfully attended every Sunday until the arrival of our first child, Ethan. Eager to get back to church, we returned when Ethan was just two week old, to listen to this dynamic pastor. During one Sunday service, a thought crossed my mind, and I pictured myself singing with the worship team. I was standing with a group of singers as we led the audience in songs. After service, I attempted to personally connect with members of the worship team, but it felt awkward to me to say, "Hey, my name is Camey, and oh, by the way, I can sing and would love to be part of the worship team too." Since putting myself out there in this scenario was not the kind of thing I would typically do, I stayed silent.

After a short time of attending the church, Nate started to volunteer in the production department, and this gave him an opportunity to have a conversation with John, the worship team director. He shared that I had a desire to serve the Lord through music and that I was gifted. This provided me with an opportunity to audition, and a few days later I was informed I had made the worship team. However, John mentioned one stipulation per the pastor's request: if I joined the team, I would have to limit my singing to only this church and wouldn't be able to sing or speak anywhere south of San Antonio (a four-hour drive north of the Valley).

Nate and I were puzzled and questioned such a restriction as we felt called to share my story wherever God allowed. We requested to meet with the pastor so he could explain the rationale behind this condition for singers. It was not typical for this pastor to meet with congregation members, but to our surprise, he agreed.

During our meeting with the pastor and John, instead of directly addressing our concerns, the pastor expressed an interest in hearing my life story. I shared my journey from childbirth onward, and his response was, "Wow, just wow! What an incredible story. You just have to share this with our church." Surprisingly, he asked if I would be willing to share it with the congregation in a couple of weeks. The excitement and joy that filled us in that moment shifted our focus away from our initial concerns and questions.

At that time, I was still working in the hospital's psychiatric unit, and my understanding of the spiritual realm was deepening. I was gaining insights into the significance of singing with authority, and the power of Jesus's blood. I discovered our new church used to be Pentecostal, and in my mind, Pentecostals were considered a lively church with flowing banners and long services filled with people raising hands, on their knees, wearing long dresses, speaking in different languages, dancing, and practicing the laying on of hands. However, this church resembled nothing like what I'd envisioned. This service was short, consisting of thirty minutes of music (about three songs) followed by a thirty-minute sermon. Every service was pre-planned and well-organized from the beginning to the end. I observed nothing unusual; only a few would raise their hands, as this church wasn't particularly focused on expressing spiritual gifts. It was a self-pronounced "seeker-friendly" contemporary church, with an emphasis on creating an environment where newcomers wouldn't be intimidated by anything perceived as strange but instead would feel a warm and welcoming atmosphere, which I believe most did.

Our son, Ethan, was just a month old when I had the opportunity to share my story and sing alongside Nate and John, and then the pastor shared a heartfelt benediction. This collective sharing unfolded across all five services, which marked a pivotal moment that solidified our connection with the church. It propelled us from being anonymous attendees to known members, prompting our progression into valued volunteer status. We felt a sense of contribution to the church, being seen, loved, and recognized by the expanding congregation.

Even though I thought I had reached my goal by becoming a member of the worship team, I still faced rejection from certain individuals. Vocalists were often given different songs to lead, and I felt as if my presence threatened their vocal opportunities to lead certain songs. Despite my genuine intentions, I began to feel excluded, which felt disappointingly familiar.

Nate, on the other hand, became more included. As the church expanded to a 2,000-member service, Nate was offered a full-time position as the technical director of the production department. This secured him a spot among the closest in the pastor's circle, which was a significant achievement for him. Meanwhile, I embraced the greatest role of my life since I was a mother to three precious boys. Ethan was born in June 2009, Caleb in June 2011, and Eli in July of 2012. The boys were born close together, which was fun, but it was a very busy season for all of us since we had three boys under the age of three. I had stopped speaking or singing south of San Antonio as requested, or really anywhere by this time, since I thought I only needed to promote and share at my local church.

I sang on the worship team most Sundays, and those were long days since I started my day around 6:00 a.m. in order to get the boys and myself ready for church. Nate was one of the first to arrive at the church at 5:30 a.m., turning on lights, and preparing all the technology that would be used during the service. Thankfully, my parents were always there to help out and watch the boys on Sundays.

This allowed me to continue my involvement on the worship team, which was a source of great joy.

As the attendance of the church grew, they hired a new teaching pastor, and his wife took over as the lead vocalist for the worship team. This shift changed the dynamics of the team, as now only John and another female leader took on the lead vocal roles while the rest of us provided background vocals, with maybe an occasional solo opportunity. The previous avoidance from my fellow team members ceased, but it wasn't a result of acceptance; rather, I was no longer perceived as a threat. I felt a mix of discouragement and envy, emotions I had never experienced in a worship setting before. The calling that God had placed on me at just five years old suddenly felt stifled, and my voice and purpose became paralyzed. It was difficult for me to even understand or express what I was feeling at that moment. Looking back, I can see that I felt as though the church was silencing my voice—specifically, my calling from God.

The female worship team leader initiated a "soul care" class with the intention of fostering closeness through sharing the deepest parts of our souls. However, my immediate observation was the leadership's reluctance to be vulnerable. The encouragement for us to open up felt one-sided, creating a sense that they were seeking an upper hand in our personal lives. It seemed like a manipulative move, as they were not reciprocating vulnerability and the sentiment remained that they were gathering information or ammunition that could potentially be used against us, all under the guise of caring for our souls.

> "A genuine worshipper's heart doesn't need the platform or microphone."

While the team was undergoing this internal turmoil, I found myself struggling with my identity as a worshipper. God, in His love, reminded me that a genuine worshipper's heart doesn't need the platform or microphone. That ministry isn't a stage but an altar. I read about King David, a worshipper in the Bible, who sought God both in the pasture and the palace. Regardless of his circumstances, he worshipped for an audience of One. As I contemplated my role on the platform, I knew I was called to be a worshipper on or off stage. An internal dialogue ensued in my mind, leading me to acknowledge that I needed to step down because I knew my heart was not right and I was spiritually unhealthy. My gift of singing was becoming an idol in my life. The focus had shifted to me, fueled by a sense of not being valued or being used, and resulted in strained interpersonal relationships. Feeling the need to prove my talents and abilities had taken a toll and proved futile.

> "Ministry isn't a stage but an altar."

What happened next felt like another moment from a movie. As I left the auditorium to pick up my kids from their classroom, a ray of light broke through the busy crowd of people leaving and coming. A short, elderly man in a classic plaid outfit with an old pocket watch in his front pocket made his way toward me, slightly out of breath as he walked with a limp.

"I'm so glad I caught you," he said, as he touched my shoulder. "I'm heading home today." He was probably a winter Texan, I thought to myself. He continued to speak. "I was hoping I would run into you to talk to you before I left. I always looked forward to seeing you on stage; it was the highlight of my Sunday. I just love, love, love to hear you worship, as it brings me so much joy."

> *My gift of singing was becoming an idol in my life.*

His words moved me, and tears pooled in my eyes. I would cry on occasion, but typically I always tried to hide my emotions in public. I wished I had expressed more to that sweet man, but all I managed to say as I stared back into his gentle eyes was, "Thank you . . . thank you . . . that means so much." As he walked away, I realized I had just encountered something truly miraculous. I wanted to find him, express more gratitude, and give him a hug for speaking to my heart, but he disappeared quickly into the crowd, and I never found him.

Throughout my history of singing on worship teams, I took many breaks when I felt that the stage was becoming more important than my love for the Lord. However, after receiving sincere encouragement which assured me I was loved and seen by the Creator of the Universe, that was enough for me. I decided to stay on the worship team as my perspective realigned with the focus of who I was singing to, making other

> *When I sing, my voice can only point to Him, the one who gave me my voice.*

recognition less important. It was a realization that when I sing, my voice can only point to Him, the one who gave me my voice.

THE OMINOUS CLIMAX

Nate was well-loved and respected as the production director at church, and I was a recognized face within the congregation. However, within the confines of our home, tensions escalated, marked by ongoing conflicts surrounding Nate's controlling and manipulative behavior and his ongoing involvement with pornography. My own well-being suffered as I too was not healthy. Often, I was fueled by a growing sense of pride and even a deceptive belief that I was somehow better than Nate because I did not share his struggles.

The recurring cycle of opposition persisted, and I sensed a constant need to fight for self-protection of my life, whether with worship team members or with Nate because I never knew if he was going to be for or against me at any particular time.

It wasn't just this ongoing conflict; Nate's job also took a toll. He was putting in long hours, typically Monday to Friday, with the occasional Saturday off. He invested fifty to sixty hours each week in preparing and orchestrating each church service and event. This was a comprehensive production involving a fifty-five-foot-wide screen, and a massive control room, as well as designing all the slides, sound and lights, and managing the entire media production staff and volunteers.

The church's growth was mirrored by the tightly knit staff who managed to handle increasing responsibilities with a small team.

Despite Nate feeling overwhelmed, the pastor took pride in accomplishing a great deal with a limited staff, often boasting of this to other pastors.

Feeling the strain, Nate approached the pastor because of his concern for the overall health of all the staff. As the father of small children, Nate realized that the time given at the church was something he could never get back, so he requested a day off on either Friday or Monday for the entire staff. The pastor's response was calculated and cold. He stated that church volunteers have a job all week and still serve on Sundays. That comment left Nate with a poignant realization and a quick rebuttal. "Volunteers can say no, but staff can't," he replied. Thankfully, a month later, the pastor reluctantly granted the staff Fridays off, but this came at a great cost to Nate as he was now seen as a potential threat to the pastor because he confronted the issue with him.

Those closest to the pastor observed a different side of him that emerged behind closed doors in meetings. It was a noticeable difference from how he presented himself on the platform. Nate and others perceived that the pastor would not be satisfied regardless of the staff's efforts; he wanted things his way. Consequently, some of the staff shifted their focus from serving God and seeking His approval to trying to please the pastor and gain his favor.

The atmosphere led to staff essentially becoming "yes men." Departing staff members who challenged the pastor or felt called elsewhere were quietly ushered out the back door, and it was understood that existing staff would not contact them.

This strain with the church combined with the strain in our relationship was streaking toward an ominous climax and impacting our spiritual well-being. A sense of underlying tension loomed, and it was taking a toll on us as we sensed things were not right at the church, yet we couldn't quite pinpoint the exact problem. A turning point occurred in the car during our return from a trip to Dallas, where we had been visiting family. I turned to Nate and expressed, "I feel like changes are coming, and we are getting ready to move." This statement resonated as a clear confirmation of what God had already conveyed to Nate during our trip in Dallas.

Upon our return to the church, I attended a friend's baby shower. As I entered the room, I immediately sensed a shift in the atmosphere. The expression on my worship director's face spoke volumes and hinted at something significant that had transpired and conveyed her displeasure. It became apparent that others were privy to more information than I was, creating an awkward and tense atmosphere.

Nate too sensed the shift with his peers as he returned to the office. The staff in his department acted strangely, offering a drawn-out "hellooooooo . . . welcome back." It was evident they knew something he didn't. After putting his things down in his office, he immediately received a call from the pastor asking him to come to his office.

In the pastor's office, the pastor began to explain the changes he made to the staff while Nate was away. "I'm taking you completely out of all service planning meetings, and you'll now be informed of the service order by John, the worship director." Nate felt perplexed and confused, experiencing what felt like a demotion. He thought, "How am I going to do a good job of running the services if I'm not even involved in the conversation?"

When the pastor asked if Nate had any questions, Nate tried to hold back his obvious confusion and frustration and simply replied, "Not really. You are the pastor and can make any changes you would like. My only concern was that all these changes were done while I was away. I just wish you would have valued the person over the decision, and that I would have been included in this conversation. Now it could appear to the rest of the staff that I did something wrong." The pastor stared at Nate for a second and then said, "I'm sorry you feel that way, but I'd do it the same again if I had to." Nate was blown away at his arrogant boldness. The pastor continued, "Nate, we all love you here, and you do amazing work, but you are just the 'get-it-done' guy. That is who you are and all you will ever be." This was the final blow, and emotionally, Nate knew this was a direct assault on what God was telling him about who he was. Nate thought, "My worth is not wrapped up in what I do or how I perform." However, he responded with an "okay," and the meeting was quickly over.

When Nate told me of the pastor's words, a sense of injustice surged within me. I didn't have the full picture or understanding, but it felt like a controlled move by the pastor to assert his authority over us. We could see that our place in the church was seemingly coming to an end, but it was also a foreshadowing of the marital issues we were about to endure. I arranged a meeting with the pastor, and surprisingly, he agreed, which again wasn't typical of him. Perhaps our history and mutual admiration allowed this meeting to happen.

The pastor's first words to me as I sat down were, "Why are you coming to me on Nate's behalf?" I explained I was concerned and unsure about how things had unfolded, seeking understanding rather than wanting to engage in a fight. The pastor, however, was guarded in his responses, making it clear that he felt no obligation to explain himself to me. I had never personally seen this defensive stance from the pastor. I had only heard about it. The tone was set, and the meeting quickly took a negative turn.

The pastor declared, "I am the pastor, and I can make decisions without being questioned," escalating the tension further. He then proceeded to attack me personally within the context of worship. "You are not even that good and don't have a soulful sound; we have others who are more qualified and talented than you." Tears welled up in my eyes because he had just verbalized exactly how I felt on the worship team, he saw my tears puddle, when I blinked the tears back. In a moment of hurt and frustration, I blurted out, "I am like a David, and you are like a Saul." The words seemed to escape my mouth without much thought, and I was shocked by their sudden emergence and boldness.

The following morning, I was previously scheduled to have breakfast with the pastor's wife, but she canceled at the last minute, mentioning that her youngest son needed her at home. Initially, this text didn't affect me much, but slowly, I connected the dots—they were done and were cutting us off. Concurrently, the worship team held an emergency meeting without my knowledge, claiming that I had requested to step down from the team. Staff members who were once close friends started distancing themselves, altering their paths to avoid me.

I was no longer on the worship team's schedule. In essence, I had been let go—fired. A burning sense of injustice consumed me, directed not just toward the pastor but the entire church team. Although I desired to expose the injustices between Nate, me, and the pastor, I knew nobody would believe me, or they would perceive me as the instigator because everyone knew the pastor could do no wrong.

I really thought Nate would be proud of me for facing the pastor and standing up for him. However, I was not prepared for Nate's response, as he became even more upset with me and felt embarrassed by my "Saul and David" analogy. He believed I was in the wrong. I felt completely isolated and weighed down by shame. I also began losing my hair, which started falling out in clumps, leaving me even more embarrassed. My world was crumbling, and my body began showing the toll it was taking.

Even after the meeting with the pastor, Nate wanted to save face and stay on staff serving the pastor. He was deeply committed to making it work, believing there would be no other job opportunity. This marked a pivotal moment when our marriage really started to crumble. It was the first time Nate emotionally withdrew from me entirely. It felt as if I didn't even know who he was. This was not the same Nate I knew, and we separated again, with him staying at my parents' house for the second time.

Nate believed from growing up in the church and because his dad was the worship pastor, that the lead pastor was anointed by God to run the church, and we were to follow without question. This belief was ingrained in him without him even fully understanding why. Nate thought he had no right to confront or challenge the pastor, let alone me. To Nate's thinking, I just needed to be more subservient.

Somehow in the midst of these chaotic circumstances, I found peace in worship that made no sense. My worship became louder than my worry, as I was confiding only in the Lord and my parents. Strangely, as difficult as it was to be let go and be removed from the team, it felt like a weight had been lifted from my shoulders. From that point forward, I no longer sat in the audience; instead, I positioned myself in the audio booth, where I was unseen, and I worshipped freely. I became what I perceived as wild, as I would dance, fall to my knees, cry, and hold nothing back from the Lord, feeling completely liberated to worship freely.

In a subsequent meeting with the pastor, without me, Nate expressed agreement with the pastor's perspective and pointed fingers at me for what had happened. Following this meeting, the church extended an olive branch by covering our expenses for a marriage intensive in Nashville, where couples went as a last resort.

We attended the entire marriage intensive with Nate telling me he was not into pornography anymore and I was an overbearing wife for not trusting him, but on the last day of the marriage intensive I learned Nate hadn't been entirely truthful about his progress and he did have an ongoing involvement with pornography.

Upon our return home, Nate still strongly desired to stay at the church, while I was not at peace with that decision. But clarity came during a scheduled production team retreat, which turned out to be distressing but made the decision to leave easy for both of us.

During the retreat, we sat in a semicircle with about twenty staff members, and the pastor went around to each person asking a specific question. Strangely, when he reached me, he skipped over without inviting me to share my thoughts, evidently intending to bypass me by going straight to Nate. Feeling exasperated, I spoke up on my own and began answering the questions, further infuriating the pastor.

Later that day we found ourselves at an outdoor mall in San Antonio. I noticed my female worship director discreetly distributing cash from an envelope to staff members. To be honest the idea of getting some spending cash was exciting, but Nate and I never received any. It appeared this was a tactic to buy off our replacements, as the pastor likely knew our time at the church was coming to an end. Although speculative, this prevailing feeling was shared by both Nate and me.

Upon our return from the retreat, Nate finally saw that the church was not fostering a healthy environment. The rose-colored glasses were gradually being lifted, revealing a reality we had not fully seen before. The solidification of this realization occurred during a meeting with the teaching pastor, whom we both greatly admired. He brought both of us in and posed a crucial question: "Are you guys all in?" Essentially, he was asking if we would go along with everything they wanted. Nate affirmed his commitment. I couldn't believe he responded yes because this was not what he was telling me at home. When the teaching pastor turned to me with the same question, my response was, "I'm going to pray about it." I could sense that my answer frustrated the pastor, as he attempted to probe deeper into my position. My continued response was, "I am going to pray about this decision," which I did.

During this period, Nate and I remained separated. Then, miraculously, we reconciled—a moment that felt like nothing less than a miracle straight from Heaven. I'm not even sure exactly how this transpired other than God was working on both of our hearts. It was during this reconciliation that Nate acknowledged his need for change, realizing that he couldn't remain in the same situation as it was leading him down paths that he no longer wanted to be on. He began exploring jobs outside of the Valley and accepted a job at a smaller church back in the DFW area. Nate submitted his two-week notice to the pastor, who was notably upset about his decision. Surprisingly Nate was granted the ability to complete a two-week transition period with the staff. However, after just one week, Nate was informed that he could leave, and his presence was no longer needed. He became yet another name on a long list of staff members who were quietly ushered out the back door.

Considering all that had transpired, I was profoundly surprised and genuinely delighted when the production and worship staff personally arranged a party for Nate and me. It was more for Nate, but I was still grateful. There had been no public announcement from the platform, not that we were looking for one, or any manner regarding our departure. We were advised to leave quietly, and the congregation had no knowledge where we went other than what I posted on social media. However, it was heartwarming to see that most members of the worship team came to say goodbye, and the entire production team was there to support Nate. They even presented us with a thoughtful and gracious farewell gift.

Notably, the lead pastor never made an appearance.

I am sincerely grateful that, despite the hurt caused by this pastor, I held onto the belief that God is still good. In my upbringing, I was fortunate to have the best pastor, and I had the opportunity to witness his character both on and off the platform—a servant, a leader, a humble man, and a teacher of the Word. That person was my dad. I now choose to no longer look through the lens of sinners to see God. I no longer hold people up to an impossible standard. Instead, I look to the goodness of God, who is perfect. I have learned not to seek validation from the church but from the Lord instead. I've learned the importance of being a servant while recognizing spiritual abuse earlier rather than later.

> "I now choose to no longer look through the lens of sinners to see God."

CHAPTER SIXTEEN
Sin Never Stays Hidden

Christmas 2014, Nate and I returned to the DFW area with our three boys, Ethan, Caleb, and Eli in tow. While we appreciated the lessons and friendships from the Valley and a newfound love for Hispanic culture, we were eager to move forward. However, it was difficult to part with our luxurious two-story home on a golf course, the first house our boys lived in, our lovely neighbors, and where we had made special memories. Due to the challenging housing market at that time, we had to sell it in a short sale without making any profit. This led us to the "temporary" two-bedroom apartment where we now lived in DFW area.

Nate's new production position at a local church provided us with a fresh start. The new church we joined brought us a breath of fresh air, distinctly opposite from the leadership we had left behind. The leadership, especially the lead pastor, displayed a genuine heart for people, which reminded me of my dad. The new pastor preached a completely different message from the one in the Valley. He expressed to staff in a meeting, "It is important that we value the person over a decision." In that moment, Nate knew we were in the right place. Nevertheless, Nate and I still carried concealed wounds from our former pastor who instructed us not to speak negatively about him since he was "God's anointed," and we never did. The wounds he inflicted ran deep, creating a scar, for both Nate and me. While we were doing our best to cope, it was obvious that we were far from being healed.

One day, a friend from high school, now also living in the bustling DFW area, excitedly invited me to her church—a massive megachurch in the heart of the metroplex. As we caught up over coffee, she mentioned a special mother's group meeting at their church. They had planned to have a time for people to pray for each other and share prophetic words from the Lord. Despite some uncertainty, I was confident in my ability to read the Bible and hear from the Lord, since He had spoken to me even as a little girl. However, I struggled to understand the significance of this prophetic appointment. I knew that the Bible, in Ephesians 2:20, says, "Together, we are his house, built on the foundation of the apostles and the prophets. And the cornerstone is Christ Jesus himself." I Corinthians 14 aslo instructs us to prophesy and encourage one another, so I felt a desperation to attend, as I knew the Lord was going to do something special.

I was running late and drove to the ladies' group in a hurry. At a stop light, I vividly recall the moment when a unique vision unfolded. In this vision, Nate, with a charismatic demeanor, stood confidently behind a pulpit, wearing a long suit coat and tie. He passionately addressed, or perhaps even preached to, a congregation of men. His words filled the room with undeniable conviction, and fervor rang out like a call to action.

I arrived at the ladies' meeting in time and was seated in a group of about eight when two ladies began to prophesy over me. Tarah, the first lady, spoke of me being a sojourner in an unfriendly land, with God bringing me to a place of peace and rest—a home, not just spiritually but a physical home that was being prepared for us. This brought excitement and encouragement, as I was starting to feel stuck in our apartment and losing hope that we would ever be able to afford a physical home again.

The second lady struggled with her words initially but then conveyed a beautiful message. She said:

> Camey, as I prayed for you, I felt like the Lord said you are like a canary on a spring morning. I can hear birds outside my window when I wake up in the morning after a long winter, and it's like, "Aww, spring is here, and I love the birds." And I felt a sense of awe—that is how the Lord feels about you. He just loves, loves, loves when you sing; it makes His heart jump and leap. I felt like He said it is the highlight of His day, that you are a warrior in singing, that you shift atmospheres and mountains move when you sing. He says yes to your request. I sense that He is so pleased with you. I felt like your heart connection is like King David; you can praise Him

like a shepherd out in the field taking care of the sheep with no one noticing, and you can praise Him in the greatest assembly, and either way, your heart is pure, and you praise Him well. Psalm 45—especially verse two says, "Grace is poured out upon your lips"—Although Psalm 45 is about Jesus, there is so much in this chapter that can also be applied to you and your life.

As her words flowed from her lips, she mentioned my heart's connection is like King David's. I couldn't contain the emotions that surged within me. Tears streamed down my cheeks in rapid succession. With trembling hands, I caught them as they dripped off my chin. It was as if the Lord himself had acknowledged or recognized my actions in the Valley. I realized, in that moment, He was with me all the time; He had never left me or forsaken me. He was there! A sense of relief and renewal washed over me like a fresh breeze, propelling me forward with renewed vigor. I felt as though my sails had been filled once again, ready to navigate the uncertain waters ahead with newfound strength and purpose. I left encouraged and amazed by my friend's church. It was at that moment my healing journey began.

When I returned home, I shared the audio recording with Nate of the encouraging word, and he, too, was moved to tears by the profound experience, knowing this was a direct sign from the Lord. However, when I excitedly recounted my daydream to Nate about him standing behind the pulpit, his response was, "That's cool that you had that daydream, but, no! I don't believe I am called to be a pastor."

STOP OR BE STOPPED

In 2016, Nate had been dealing with a persistent cold for two weeks. Initially, we both thought he could overcome it without antibiotics since he didn't have a fever and his cough seemed to be fading. But then, he began complaining about intense soreness in his left quadriceps, and massaging the area provided only minor relief.

Over the next couple of days, his right leg became sore, akin to a charley horse or the feeling after an intense workout. It became difficult for him to lift his leg into our SUV as he had to use his upper body strength to pull himself up.

On Palm Sunday, Nate woke up around 3:00 a.m. and then woke me up, convinced something wasn't right. He suspected he might be having a heart attack. Initially, I thought it might be an anxiety attack, as he often worked himself up before a major event at church, so I encouraged him to relax. Checking his elevated heart rate and blood pressure, I advised him to go back to bed and let me know if his symptoms worsened. I was skeptical at first, thinking he might be exaggerating.

An hour later, he urgently woke me up by exclaiming, "Camey, I can't move. Something's not right!" Hearing a crash, I realized he had fallen off the bed in an attempt to stand up and was now lying on the floor unable to get up. After a lengthy struggle on the floor, where he wiggled back and forth, Nate somehow managed to get his legs under him and make it to the shower. Initially,

I was reassured that he was doing better. However, things took a drastic turn.

Nate texted Dr. Jay, our brother-in-law, but Dr. Jay had left his phone downstairs and didn't see the text. Miraculously, my parents were staying at Jay and Shannon's house that night and were downstairs when the text came through. My dad noticed the message, and promptly woke Jay to show it to him. Jay immediately called Nate and listened as he explained his symptoms. Jay replied, "I think you may have Guillain-Barré, and you need to go to the emergency room immediately." Dad then rushed to pick up Nate to transport him to the hospital. Miraculously, Nate managed to navigate down the long flight of stairs at our apartment with the assistance of my dad. Jay met them at the hospital, where Nate was promptly admitted and placed in a bed for evaluation. At this point, Nate lost his ability to move his lower extremities for four days. He underwent MRIs and was, indeed, later diagnosed with Guillain-Barré Syndrome (GBS) in its early stages and received IV immunoglobulin therapy. The therapy, costing around $75,000 to $100,000 per treatment, was miraculously covered by insurance. A gracious church member generously covered the deductible of approximately $2,500, which we did not have at that time. Nate remained in the hospital for seven days before finally being released. I, of course, was worried after having read on the internet that some individuals succumb to this medical complication. Ironically, my current PRN job was serving as a home health nurse, administering IVIG therapy to patients with GBS and stiff person syndrome.

While Nate still experiences occasional flare-ups from GBS, he now manages them with IgG powder, thanks to Dr. Jay's recommendation. This has been a lifesaver, allowing him to regain strength within one to three days of reoccurrence. Despite Nate's physical recovery, our marriage was crashing. His illness didn't magically improve our circumstances, and we fell back into familiar patterns or cycles of betrayal, arguments, making up, and then back to betrayal again.

Shortly after Nate's hospitalization, one year since I received the encouraging prophetic word about moving into a physical home, Nate found a four-bedroom house that exceeded our budget—a charming older home that had undergone complete remodeling the previous year. It turned out to be the perfect fit for our family. To our amazement, the owner accepted our initial bid, which was below the asking price, sealing the deal.

We learned the day after signing the sales contract that the owner had received a bid well above his asking price, and we were reminded once again that this was a moment of fulfilled promises, and we were grateful for the turn of events. Thank you, Lord, for our new home.

DAD'S OPEN HEART

In 2018, my dad faced an unexpected life-threatening triple bypass open heart surgery. Driving nine hours through the night to south Texas, I was fervently praying that my dad would be okay. I arrived the morning before his procedure. Something this traumatic would have typically been very hard for me to hear, but several months earlier, my parents joined Nate and me for a prayer session. The words of Wendy and Stephen echoed in my mind during the drive to the Valley. Without knowing my parents, Wendy prophesied:

> So Rea, what I heard was you are a man after God's heart. You have a spirit like David—a warrior, yet gentle. You know how to wield your sword in the heavenlies, taking out the enemy. Yet, you wear an apron and a towel in service to others, and the Lord just loves you and is so proud of you. You flow in every gift. Are you a pastor? You have the Father's heart, and you are so gentle. You and Judi have been so gentle with people, and yet, in the heavenlies, you are mighty warriors. You have taken the enemy out for so many people, hitting the mark and pulling out the fiery darts that the enemy has shot. Healing comes in, and you speak His Word with accuracy, flowing in the prophetic as you hear from the throne room. I heard the Lord say they have experienced great loss, but I am so pleased, so proud of them, as they count it all for His glory. You have trusted the Lord as you have been stretched further than most, and you have proved faithful. You bring the Lord glory. I want to honor you in what you have done to advance His Kingdom here on Earth and the way you have reached people all around the world

is beautiful. I hear the Lord say, "Don't fear," don't fear anything, because I hear the Lord say He's got you, engraved on the palm of His hands. He will never leave you or forget you.

Then Stephen followed:

In Nehemiah, it says the joy of the Lord will be your strength. I sense there is a joy that is continually making you stronger. Then he read Isaiah 40:30–31, and I feel Rea you have a Caleb spirit. There are mountains still to climb, there are giants still to conquer, and God is renewing your strength to accomplish more. God is saying He's not done with you, Rea. There is so much more I have for you to do, but not by power, not by might, but by His Spirit, says the Lord. The Lord is giving you a fresh spirit to renew your strength to climb those mountains and to take out those giants for the Lord.

Wendy added:

Speaking of Nehemiah, the Lord reminded me he is a builder. He is an apostolic builder who has planted so many institutions of worship for Him around the world, and you have so much more to build. So He is going to give you strength and the ability. You have always availed yourself, and He's always made you able, and that's the future.

These words resonated in my heart—there are more mountains to climb, more giants to fight, and more to build—giving me hope my dad was going to live and not die! And make it he did; his surgery didn't come without obstacles, but he did great, and he still continues to build as he serves others.

GLUTTON FOR PUNISHMENT

I don't know what compelled me to go back, but in 2018, I visited our former church while visiting my dad during his surgery. Was it because I missed the people? Was I like a battered spouse going back to an abusive relationship? Did I hope to see old friends or face our old pastor? My exact reasoning eluded me, but deep down, I harbored no ill will toward our old church, pastor, or anyone there. My heart held nothing but forgiveness. I attended a Wednesday night service, where typically the teaching pastor, whom Nate and I admired, would make the Bible come alive. To my shock, our old pastor walked onto the stage in all his glory—tall, with eloquent speech, the same pastor I remembered. He immediately fixed his gaze on me. At one point, I decided to take out my camera to snap a picture; he saw me, and it appeared as if he were striking a pose for the photo in my direction.

The sermon that followed was exceptionally good, and I recall each point vividly as I took impeccable notes. His words felt eerily familiar, each point directly paralleling our experiences, almost as if he were speaking directly to me. After concluding his sermon, the pastor left the stage, which would be the last I would ever see him. Older staff members, whom I knew well, gathered around me after the conclusion of the service. I hugged everyone but turned to my old worship team directors and expressed, "I felt like his sermon was aimed at me." The female worship pastor nonchalantly said, "Oh, no . . . I don't think so, he would never do that."

On my way home, I recounted everything to Nate on the phone, and he affirmed, "Yep, he's done that many times before, as I have seen him while in the control room. He tailors his illustrations and sermon notes based on who's in the room." What was even more telling was that the online sermon was entirely different from the one he'd delivered that evening.

I am a loyal person. I followed our old pastor and listened to his sermons for many years after leaving the church. But the minute I left that day, I decided to never listen to another one of his sermons again. It set the boundary of, "I forgive him, but I owe him nothing," and it was then I broke all ties. I no longer owed him loyalty and no longer allowed him to continue to have power or control over me.

In the years that followed, Nate and I both began to understand the abusive nature of that situation and how our thinking had become warped in the way we served others, particularly in the context of spiritual leadership. We saw firsthand how easy it was to be manipulated, trapped within the four walls of a church, all the while losing our calling.

Believing I had reconciled myself to damage done, we were delivered a severe blow. The worship pastor, who had been at the church for eighteen years, finally decided to leave. He reached out to Nate to reconnect and shared with him that the pastor had made the disturbing claim to his inner staff that I was demon-possessed. Nate relayed those accusing words to me as I was heading into work. I pulled over, stopped my car, hit my steering wheel, and let out a cry of lament. I was utterly shattered. I was furious that he would spew lies about me, while telling us not to talk about "God's anointed." I was saddened by the thought that my friends would believe him. Yet, the question remained: Was I really that surprised? Truthfully no; unfortunately, I wasn't surprised at all.

> He was removing my need for approval or self-recognition, a need to prove myself to others because He already approved of me!

Sitting in my car, my prayer was simple: "Lord, fight my battles and let the truth reign." Then, as in Psalm 109, when David implores God for justice over his accusers, I said, "Let every curse he's spoken over me be returned."

Suddenly, it was as if I could understand the lessons God was teaching me. I am more than just a singer on a worship team; I am a worshipper. He was removing my need for approval or self-recognition, a need to prove myself to others because He already approved of me! Scars were beginning to fade.

UNHEALTHY CYCLES

I never knew how Nate was going to react whenever I tried to discuss his involvement with pornography. Our disagreements tended to escalate rapidly, starting from a previous argument, characterized by raised voices, physical tension, and accusations. Our arguments followed a familiar pattern. Nate's constant belittling jabs toward me always left me feeling torn and conflicted. While I wanted to stand up for myself and speak my mind, I would sometimes withdraw into silence or give in to Nate's demands to argue. It was a never-ending cycle of frustration and hurt. When our arguments happened in front of the kids, it only added to the turmoil inside me. How could I continue living like this?

Following the exposure of lies, I would resort to shaming and belittling. In those moments, a sense of fear would creep over me that this could escalate to physical or emotional harm. Although physical harm was never a real threat, my emotional well-being was on shaky ground. I held onto grudges and withheld affection, while Nate consistently apologized. However, I had grown weary of hearing apologies. What I truly desired was to witness a genuine change of heart.

While he apologized, the word sorry wasn't in my vocabulary, possibly because I seldom felt at fault. This was a most defiant prideful stance. When I did apologize (which was a rare occurrence), I genuinely meant it from the depths of my soul.

Another concern that weighed heavy on me was that I knew, from previous experiences, Nate would paint inaccurate narratives of me to those closest to me and or to his family, which caused me more fear of being inaccurately judged and, in turn, resulted in further anxiety.

Over the years, I observed a transformation in myself. Once characterized by joy and extroversion, I shifted toward introversion and increased self-consciousness. While my inner joy persisted, I found myself withdrawing from social interactions, smiling less, and deviating from my usual role as the "life of the party." Attending social events became less appealing, a departure from my typical demeanor. I became more self-preoccupied with my perceived failing looks, from my thinning hair to my skin breaking out.

Nate's wandering eye and flirtations with other women were always on my radar, causing deep distress as I had no way to prove or stop his behavior. I would always notice the "attractive girl" in the room first, as I was almost certain he would lock eyes with her at some point. My concerns were often dismissed with responses like, "You're overreacting; I wasn't looking at her, I was looking at fill-in-the-blank." During this time, my anger and fear coexisted, alongside the fear of abandonment—which loomed large. My dependence on Nate for all aspects of my life intensified my paranoia of feeling trapped, as he took charge of everything from phone accounts, computer accounts, home finances, bank accounts, and passwords.

As a result, I took on a Sherlock Holmes-like role, always on the lookout to "catch" Nate in the act. Always giving him false demands: "If I ever catch you again, we are done. I am done. I will leave you." This likely scratches the surface, but our relationship's cycle proved unhealthy to say the least.

A pervasive sense of an unspoken third party hung over our relationship, marked by secrecy, concealed actions, and dishonesty. I oscillated between feeling responsible for Nate's struggles, entertaining thoughts that I fell short of his expectations because of my reactions, talents, and looks, to shifting the blame entirely onto him. Throughout it all, I consistently yearned for honesty, valuing it over the pervasive deception in our relationship. I wanted the truth.

THE JUDGE

By this point, after having been married for fourteen years, I felt like I had fought for our relationship long enough and I was ready to throw in the towel. Years before, I had started reading a book that proved too emotionally intense to complete. However, upon learning about a movie adaptation in the works, I decided to give it a watch. The film and the book had been highly controversial within Christian circles, and I can see both perspectives of the story. However, God used this movie to speak into my life, and it had a profound impact on me. One pivotal scene featured the main character challenging God, questioning why a horrible act had happened to his child. The main character now firmly believed the perpetrator deserved death, serving a just punishment for his sins. Eventually, the main character finds himself in the judgment seat judging others, only then understanding the impact of his own judgmental behavior his whole life. Through this experience, he learns that God is just and loving, but we live in a fallen world where pain and sin exist, and we are not God.

Tears flowed from the depths of my soul as memories flooded my mind—moments where I played the role of a judge over Nate,

> **I recognized my unworthiness to judge others and realized the harsh lens I used on them was the same through which I judged myself.**

mean girls at school, nursing colleagues, and fellow church members. It dawned on me—I had no right to pass judgment on anyone. I recognized my unworthiness to judge others and realized the harsh lens I used on them was the same through which I judged myself.

START WALKING

When we first moved back to Dallas, I heard these specific words from the Lord, which I shared with Nate: "The church is not the four walls. You are the church, and I am calling you to walk." Neither of us knew exactly what that meant, but we were in a season of wrestling with the Lord. We felt like the Israelites wandering in the wilderness, and we began questioning our place in our current ministry. We weren't happy and felt stuck in our calling, especially in our marriage, yet church ministry was all we knew, having both grown up in the church and having served within its four walls. Yet, it was here in this wilderness season I would learn a very valuable lesson.

One day, Nate distinctly heard the Lord say, "Start walking." Not sure about the meaning or where to go, Nate received a call from our brother-in-law Jay the next day. Jay told Nate that God had told him to hire him at his thriving medical practice in Southlake, Texas. Nate wasn't expecting to leave the local church, but because of the word he received the day before, he asked to pray about this decision. It became clear to both of us that God was up to something, and despite the initial fear of leaving the comfort of what we knew, we felt peace about this move.

Nate scheduled a meeting with the pastors. He expressed our desire to leave well, determined not to repeat the same test that led us there. The church was very gracious, allowing Nate to serve an extra three months to transition his position well, which would take us to the end of that year. Unbeknownst to us, this transition to working outside of the four walls of the church would allow Nate to later minister even more, by mentoring men and walking with them in discipleship. We were determined to thrive in our transition. However, we weren't prepared for the fact that this was a step into one of the darkest times of our marriage.

D-DAY

On December 3, 2016, as I stood outside my house, I was listening to a soulful rendition of "Oh Holy Night," and the third verse struck me like a lightning bolt: "Chains shall He break, for the slave is your brother, and in His Name, all oppression shall cease." I raised my hands, and tears began to stream down my cheeks. It was as if I could no longer remain standing, so I knelt down in front of our home.

For a split second, I questioned if I might be acting a bit foolish, and I went back inside. I entered my kitchen area and knelt down, and a wail began to billow out from the depths of my soul—a sound I had never heard before. It was then that I heard the Lord ask if I trusted Him. Without hesitation, I responded with a resounding "Yes, yes, Lord, I trust You." He then told me to give all of it to Him, and in that moment—I gave it all to Him. I could no longer be Nate's God or judge; I could no longer judge anyone for that matter. In that moment, I released the control I had held onto and surrendered, turning over my personal power so I could receive the healing I desperately needed. I made the conscious decision to trust God with everything from that day forward.

Little did I know God was preparing for what lay ahead later that evening. As with all things, truth always wins and will always prevail.

After Nate returned home, his open computer lay on our bed. I was trying to resist the urge to snoop, but I felt a nudge. With a click, I discovered a multitude of concerning links and pornography. I quickly took a picture of the computer before I confronted Nate. He dismissed my concerns as usual. Calmly, which was different from my usual presentation when catching him in the act, I presented the photo I had taken. Speechless, he ended his attempts at manipulation. That night, he slept on the couch, a customary response to such revelations.

The following day, I had scheduled to record a video at church addressing Christmas. I spoke these words into a camera:

> If I'm being honest, this season of life has been really difficult, one in which the enemy almost took me out. I was like, "I'm done, I'm done." But the Lord reminded me that He can use you in different seasons of your life in the good and the bad. God's got you, and in every season of life, there is only one name that, even the mention or whisper of, His

Name the enemy has to leave, and the mountain in front of you has to move, and the chains have to break. There is one name who holds all authority and all power, and that name is the name of Jesus.

I was saying this as I concealed my decision to finally file for divorce. Feeling lost, I focused on practical steps—dealing with bank accounts that I had no knowledge of, transferring money into a secret account, and searching for divorce lawyers. As I sifted through a cluttered drawer in search of a sticky note to jot down some numbers, I stumbled upon something unexpected. Instead of the usual sticky notes, I pulled out a card that caught my attention—it read "Marriage Ministry." Instantly, memories of receiving prayer from this trusted church flashed through my mind. With a bit of hesitation, I made up my mind to dial the number right then and there.

I called and spoke with a compassionate woman named Crystal. I poured out my struggles—failed counseling attempts; Nate's manipulations, sly words, and his ability to win people over; and finally, our roles working in ministry. Crystal listened attentively and then asked if she could pray over me. I agreed, since I was only upset with Nate and not with the Lord, and as she prayed, a sense of peace overwhelmed me. Her beautiful prayer left me speechless; it was her words that filled me with awe. I felt power as she prayed, but also her empathy, kindness, gentleness, and love. Her prayer became the catalyst for my decision to give our marriage one final, desperate attempt, even though deep down, I feared it was already over. I expressed my weariness with superficial approaches, and she resonated with that, understanding exactly what would be best for our next steps.

Only later did I learn that she and her husband had faced and overcome similar challenges. Her story stands as a testament that miracles still exist today. Because of what she had walked through and conquered, she possessed specific keys to victory, and she held authority to help unlock these same doors in our marriage.

CHAPTER SEVENTEEN
Life After Death
(MARRIAGE 911)

Nate and I decided to enroll in the marriage classes Crystal had recommended. I believe Nate was enthusiastic about the prospect of a second start, while I wasn't quite sure about my feelings. Nevertheless, I resolved to give the first class a chance. Yet having been through countless failed attempts to fix broken cycles, I wasn't holding my breath.

On the first night of class, Pastor Liz entered—a beautiful, lively, and confident woman. As she shared her own marriage story, I noticed that it resembled ours in many ways. I felt an immediate connection with her as she skillfully articulated her struggles, wounds, and scars, without letting the scars define her or allowing them to take her calling away. As we sat there, captivated by her words, I was almost certain that our mouths were agape in awe. Her transparency was like a melody, and with each harmonious note, it felt as if walls were beginning to crumble. It was her relatable narrative that drew me back the following night.

These classes aimed to strengthen marriages and not point the finger or harm spouses, but rather get to the root of deception and betrayal, deepening the relationship with God, which leads to healing and freedom.

Liz wouldn't allow Nate to sweet talk his way around his issues while pointing the finger at me, and she wouldn't allow me to act out from my anger and fears. She could see right through both of us, cutting through the lies to our core, straight to the real disguised issues. Her insights became our miracle, a trusted source for both of us. We looked forward to each session as we heard stories of betrayal from other couples, most of whom had worked in ministry. It was sad, yet it was comforting knowing Nate and I were not alone.

NATE'S TRANSFORMATION

Through this class, I discovered that Nate, like me, carried unseen wounds—scars that I either didn't notice or, frankly, didn't want to acknowledge. Nate had a constant fear of falling short in the eyes of family and peers, wounds from a very young age. He earned accolades through his pursuit of perfectionism, steering clear of criticism at all costs. The idea of exposure struck at the core of his being, especially since he prided himself on being the good guy. His typical responses involved resistance to any exposure, with denial, minimization, partial truths, controlling behavior of the narrative, and then like an elite basketball player, he would pivot trying to please me at all costs. He would go into ultra-please mode, getting me whatever I wanted or needed in an attempt to manipulate me right back into the same old cycle. While I truly believed he didn't want to live this way, the truth is, addiction always leads to lies and more lies in an attempt to cover up the original lie. There is no cure, only freedom from the bondage.

After any exposure of bad behavior, Nate would immerse himself in reading the Bible and self-help books, but unfortunately, these efforts rarely lasted more than a few weeks, and he would revert to his previous patterns.

It wasn't until one of our meetings with Liz that she clarified a crucial concept for Nate, helping him understand my perspective. He finally understood that his apologies alone didn't make me feel safe. Liz shared how she felt secure when her husband was in a healthy spiritual place—a sentiment I wholeheartedly agreed with. Memories of my dad reading his Bible in the early morning hours had left a lasting impression on me. Our former teaching pastor in the Valley always emphasized that he had never met a man who was struggling with an addiction who was also actively and passionately in the Word each day. The two just don't go together. Not to say we all don't struggle with temptation, but being committed to Scripture and leading a hidden, or double life, just couldn't coexist.

During this time, I witnessed Nate's apologies transforming into actions as he actively sought the Lord every morning before any of us were awake. It was there, alone in his chair, that he cried to the Lord in desperation. He realized it wasn't about salvaging our marriage but about surrendering to God. It was then that he heard the Lord speak clearly, "Camey has never been the problem." Nate had wrongly used my expression of anger or frustration to justify his struggle with pornography, convincing himself that if only I were less angry or less critical, or treated him more kindly, he wouldn't turn to pornography. The words God spoke to him at that moment were filled with love; they were not condemning or accusatory. It was like a father speaking to his child, saying, "I understand, my son. I see what's happening. I see where you're hiding, and there's a better way."

He would also give me space. Instead of chasing me around, he would simply say, "I am here to talk whenever you're ready," or he would ask me, "What can I do to make you feel safe?" It was important to him to work on himself because he didn't like how this behavior made me feel.

From that day forward, Nate killed every idol he had built that kept him away from the Lord and submitted completely to Him. He switched to a flip phone, removed all social media accounts, and installed an accountability filter on his computer. He also gave me access to everything. He let go of control and embraced change, signifying a true transformation. His actions spoke louder than any apology, and they altered the course of our marriage. Curious about what prompted the change, I asked him. He shared that reading the Bible had helped him understand the heart of his Father. He also had read a book titled, Killing Kryptonite: Destroy What Steals Your Strength, which taught him the importance of not just struggling through addiction or hiding it, but actively destroying it. To achieve this, he needed to submit himself to the Lord, ridding himself of all that he was tightly holding on to and striving to no longer hide his actions. "Camey," he said, "For the first time, I opened our front door and began commanding every evil spirit within me to come up and out. I commanded every evil thing I had given access to in my life to leave and never return. This was new to me, but I felt a shift within me. I knew I was dying to myself in every way." I can testify, Nate had truly been changed.

MY TRANSFORMATION

As I witnessed a profound transformation in Nate, his heart exuded purity, and his love for me became unmistakably evident. I started to feel safe around him. I began to trust his words and stopped trying to decipher whether what he was saying was in fact the truth. Seeing Nate's newfound zeal for the Lord, something I had never seen before, sparked excitement for our future. Liz emphasized the necessity of laying bare every hidden aspect and every deception in our marriage in order for our marriage to thrive. I confess that when I started to tell my story, it came from a place of deep wounding, and I yearned for healing, sought forgiveness, and I too wanted to be set free.

While I had previously come to understand I was acting self-righteously and judging, I hadn't had my full change of heart, like Nate. I still judged, I still felt self-righteous, and I harbored a secret.

Before Nate's spiritual transformation, I vividly remember driving to work one day when I openly expressed, "Lord, I have never had, and I never will have, an issue with lust." I even ventured further to imply this thought, "I don't think Satan could even trap me in this particular area." While I may have felt a twinge of reservation for speaking so frankly, I was proud of my steadfast heart and my ability to overcome any challenges in this regard.

After voicing such a self-righteous prayer, I began to feel a target on my back with an invisible bullseye signaling others to approach from all directions. It began with fleeting glances from across the room at my kid's school, actions I initially dismissed. However, one particular gaze stood out, making me feel uncomfortable and self-conscious. Questions swirled in my mind, causing me to question why this man had stared at me. Was he staring because of the color of my skin? Because of my scars? Had he ever encountered someone with a cleft or noticeable scars before? I didn't see myself as conventionally pretty, so I doubted that was his reason.

Days turned into weeks, weeks into months, and months into years and things progressed.

I became hyperaware and increasingly sensitive to the glances, engaging in a silent game of whether he was staring at me or not. The awareness grew to the point where I found myself subtly checking to see where he was in a room. Our eyes would occasionally meet, leading to moments of embarrassment as I didn't want him to misinterpret my actions—I was merely gauging whether he was looking at me. Although this guy didn't fit my type or compare to Nate in any way, I never shared these encounters with him. It wasn't that I consciously chose to keep it a secret; rather, I didn't give it much thought.

Then the intensity of the looks escalated to awkward conversations, small exchanges that occurred occasionally. Then came the compliments—not spoken directly to me but to my husband. "Wow,

Camey has such great style; she could wear anything." Hearing these compliments, I felt a flutter in my heart, appreciating that someone thought I was attractive. Eventually, the compliments bypassed my husband and were directed at me personally. He would come up behind me, touch my long hair that cascaded down to my lower back, and whisper something in my ear as he smelled my hair. "I love that jacket." I felt a shiver run down my body with his touch, and in that moment, I realized he had captured a part of my heart, or so I thought.

As time went on, I couldn't comprehend how others, especially Nate, failed to see the reality of what was truly happening. One day, I arrived early at school to drop off supplies. He spotted me and made a beeline directly to me with open arms for a full-on frontal hug. In the typical "Christian" world, greetings between men and women were often limited to the friendly "side hug" to prevent any indecency between a man and woman. However, this embrace made me feel seen and loved, something I hadn't experienced in a long time. During this time I felt Nate was distant emotionally and was unable to offer any sense of security. After this drawn-out hug, his wife entered the building, and our eyes met, but he remained oblivious to her gaze, as he was facing the opposite direction. Attempting to extricate myself from the hug proved challenging as he just held onto me longer. I didn't feel it was a lustful hug at that time, but his wife was visibly upset, and I knew it was inappropriate. Nate, unaware, considered us all friends at this point.

Believing everything was okay, I allowed connecting through texting about school matters, but gradually, our conversations shifted from educational topics to more personal discussions. We even extended our connection to social media, exchanging hundreds of likes and hearts as he became my number-one fan. As our friendship deepened, a thought crossed my mind: "If things don't work out with Nate, I could envision settling down with him. The boys love him, and I feel everything would be okay."

One day after school, my kids didn't come out at their usual time in the car line, and it was over thirty minutes after their release, so I started to panic a little. With rain starting to drizzle, I parked and ran from my car to the side door of the school when I bumped into him in between cars. He caught me, gently touched my arms, and said, "Mrs. Armstrong, I wanted to talk to you for a second." In my mind, I knew I was in a hurry to grab the kids, but I stopped. He said he really loved my oldest son, Ethan, so much and wanted Ethan to be on his basketball team. Staring into his deep eyes, I totally forgot his question, as I think he did too. The rain began to pour, he leaned in closer, closer to me as if to protect me from the rain. We were not a hand's distance away, eye to eye and face to face when a loud thunderclap roared and shook me. Just then, I stepped back and started walking backward to the side door, yelling, "Thanks, I'll talk to Ethan and let you know." He stood motionless in the rain between the cars.

Yes, I was actually that close to having ruined everything in my marriage, which would have solidified Nate's and my decision to get a divorce.

The summer came and went, and I did not see this man because my kids changed schools. We continued to correspond through social media and he would comment on how amazing I looked, but it was over. And once I realized I was playing with fire that I had no business playing with, I stopped engaging. I felt, at the time, I was justified because of what Nate had been doing to me, but I learned that two wrongs don't make a right.

A crucial moment occurred when a beautiful high school student, dressed in a tight maroon outfit that left little to the imagination, walked right in front of him. Instead of merely noticing, he exclaimed, "Wow, you look beautiful. I just love that outfit on you!" A flood of emotions engulfed me—anger, jealousy, and a profound sense of betrayal. I recognized the familiar sting of betrayal, and it hurt deeply. It became clear to me right then and there that he was no better than Nate, betraying not only me but also his wife. It was a stark realization that I, too, had unwittingly become the other woman.

From that moment onward, I turned to God in prayer, seeking Him to make things right. My prayers extended not only to his wife, fervently wishing for the strength and restoration of their marriage, but also for Nate and me. Recognizing this situation had gone too far, I felt an urgency to put an end to it. However, I questioned how to stop it. Despite my prayers, I sensed either they weren't being heard or I lacked the strength in my human flesh to halt this course of events.

My memory flashed back to me sitting in my car emphatically declaring to God that I would never struggle with lust nor could ever be tempted to stray from Nate. It was then that I gained a deeper understanding of Nate's struggle with pornography and how easily one could become ensnared. Then another mom, my friend, observed the subtle exchange of glances between him and me. I believed it was a secret shared only between us, but my friend knew what was transpiring. While I was aware that she knew, she never directly addressed the situation with me.

Recognizing again the need for change, I hesitated to inform Nate directly. Instead, I convinced myself that I could handle it independently, downplaying the situation as "not that big of a deal" since nothing physical had occurred. Here I was making excuses, downplaying, and hiding . . . sound familiar?

Years down the road, my rose-colored glasses have been removed by Nate, and my forgiveness glasses have been placed on by Jesus. I never felt condemnation from Nate ever. I even wondered if he knew what I was saying because he was so calm hearing every detail. I, too, allowed Nate to read and have access to every text, while secretly wanting him to feel the pain of betrayal as I so often had felt. But the more I spilled, the more grace he gave. Nate became the bigger man, spiritually. He does not carry any ill will toward the other man—none. Nate and I have learned that having a "best" or "special" friend of the opposite sex while married will never work. It just can't happen. Why? Because your best friend should always be your spouse.

PART III

CHAPTER EIGHTEEN

Dreams

Entering this new chapter, Nate and I found ourselves prospering in our relationship, not just with each other but also more importantly with God. We intentionally positioned God at the top, forming a triangle with Nate and me on the outer edges at the bottom. What's truly beautiful is that as we drew nearer to God, we also grew closer together.

While preparing to speak in Houston, I was reminded of a dream.

~

While on a plane and preparing for a connecting flight, the flight attendant approached me before takeoff, requesting my boarding pass. It dawned on me that I had inadvertently left my ticket at the terminal.

The flight attendant insisted I couldn't board the next flight without proof of my ticket. I felt frustration bubbling up, especially since I had been allowed on without it previously. Resigned to the situation, I retraced my steps and located my ticket where I had left it. Despite the delay, I returned to the flight attendant, presenting my ticket as evidence. "Look," I said, "I had it all along, just forgot to bring it with me."

~

In this dream, I came to a realization: Often, we find ourselves attempting to prove or validate our calling, abilities, and gifts, to others. However, when God calls, He validates, eliminating the need for external validation or proof of our calling. The reassuring truth is Jesus already has our seat reserved and is calling us to our next plane and destination.

He's your ticket! Get on the right plane and don't confuse man's rejection for God's rejection. As stated in 1 Peter 5:6–7 (MSG), "So be content with who you are and don't put on airs. God's strong hand is on you; he'll promote you at the right time. Live carefree before God; he is most careful with you."

~

With this new revelation, opportunities began coming to me without seeking them out, allowing me the chance to share my story. As doors opened, I found myself going to prisons, retreats, and meeting people in the streets, grocery stores, and restaurants. I was reaching people who were bleeding and dying due to wounds inflicted by the church, pastors, or by people who professed to believe in Jesus but lacked the essential fruit of love, joy, peace, patience, goodness, kindness, and self-control. These wounded people were in desperate need of the real love of Jesus.

BUCKET LIST TRIP

Emerging from the confines of the respiratory illness lockdown, Nate stumbled upon his dream vacation to Fiji. He found a tempting deal for an entire week for two at an all-inclusive, luxurious resort including airfare, for only $2,900! It was an offer too good to refuse, so Nate seized the opportunity.

We flew 6,629 miles to reach the beautiful paradise islands of Fiji. Upon our arrival, we were immediately met by torrential rain. This added an unexpected twist to our adventure that was just beginning. We took a bus, navigating through what seemed like rivers masquerading as roads, as the water reached above its large tires.

When we arrived at our resort, the rain had mercifully ceased. Nate, ever the planner, was so excited about an excursion he had booked for the next day to a distant island—a day promised to be filled with scuba diving, snorkeling, and encounters with crystal-clear waters. He was hopeful that his plans wouldn't be ruined.

As we entered the hotel, chaos ensued in the lobby. Hundreds of guests, some visibly upset, were frantically rescheduling their flights and plans, creating a bustling scene. The front desk, in a state of panic, informed us of an unknown wait before we could access our room. Drawing from his experience in the hotel industry, Nate skillfully negotiated an upgrade. Soon enough, we found ourselves upgraded to a private bungalow by the water, turning an unforeseen delay into a luxurious experience. Later when we made our way to the dining area, we were again met with a scene of scattered people and informed that the wait would be a staggering four hours! As we stood in line, we struck up a conversation with a friendly couple from Australia, who dropped a bombshell—a cyclone was expected to hit later that night. Shocked and uninformed, we realized that our much-anticipated bucket list trip might turn into a real "wash."

Nate, sensing the impending disappointment, shared our predicament with the couple we had just met. When their name was called for a dinner table, they graciously invited us to join them, adjusting the reservation from two to four. We enjoyed a delightful dinner together, as we listened to the pounding of wood being placed over the windows of the resort. They empathized with our situation, understanding that our vacation plans were now in shambles due to the approaching cyclone.

They gave us a number for a driver named Dan, vouching that he would be an awesome tour guide who could show us around Fiji once the rain subsided. We were trapped in our room for two consecutive days, listening to the relentless howling of the wind and the pounding rain. Despite his frustration, Nate managed to reschedule our excursion, pending better weather. In the meantime, I decided to reach out to Dan for a day-long exploration of the beautiful island. As the phone rang and rang, I noticed that Dan's ringtone was not your ordinary sound; instead, I was listening to the song, "What a Beautiful Name." I immediately knew he loved Jesus. Convinced, I insisted to Nate that when we met Dan, we should have his pastor pray over us. To this, Nate wholeheartedly agreed. Dan returned our call the next day and was excited at the opportunity to show us around his beautiful country after the storm.

After enduring three days of incessant rains and winds, finally, the clouds parted, and the sun came out. We were seated in the dining area, overlooking a murky ocean, not the anticipated crystal-clear waters that Fiji is known for. I randomly asked Nate, "What was your word for this year?" After a long pause, I then blurted out, "My word is power!"

The next day as we were riding with Dan, I wasted no time in expressing my desire to meet his pastor. The request caught him off guard since he had never had this request from a resort guest. A hint of hesitation crossed his face, possibly due to concerns about sharing personal information. However, after a moment, he agreed but reluctantly added, "Well, my pastor is a little different. He will not only know about your past, but he will also speak into your future." Excitedly, I responded, "Yes! That is the one we need to meet! As long as your pastor loves Jesus and is a disciple."

Everything was starting to come together as we drove across the island witnessing the breathtaking landscapes of Fiji, reminiscent of the beauty of Guatemala with its majestic mountains and lush green trees. The people we encountered were nothing short of amazing—kind, loving, giving, and gracious. They often greeted us with "Bula," which is not just a greeting; it carries a profound meaning as it translates to "life." When Fijians say "Bula" to each other, they are essentially conveying the essence of life. The sheer beauty of the land and its people overwhelmed my heart during my visit there.

The following day, we successfully embarked on our scheduled excursion, and although the water conditions may not have been optimal due to the recent cyclone, it was undeniably stunning; the water under the surface was crystal clear and breathtaking. The pinnacle of our vacation unfolded on the last day when we were scheduled to meet Dan's pastor, Viliame (Pastor Vili for short).

As we pulled up to Pastor Vili's home, a sense of uncertainty lingered in the air. We waited for a while in Dan's car, unsure if the meeting had been scheduled or if the pastor was even aware of our visit. Then to our excitement, Pastor Vili arrived accompanied by another pastor, creating a somewhat awkward moment as Dan got out of his car to talk with the other pastor while Pastor Vili sat in the front passenger seat of Dan's car. Nate was in the driver's seat, and I sat in the back, recording the conversation on my phone.

Pastor Vili began by sharing that he had originally planned to meet another pastor for coffee when God told him that two pastors (referring to us) were waiting in front of his home. Without hesitation, they left their coffee plans and rushed to meet us, apologizing for any delay.

Pastor Vili then began recounting his own story, generously opening up to Nate and me:

> It's an extraordinary testimony of how I transformed from a troubled youth, one who was running from the Lord, to becoming a mighty man of God. During my upbringing, I engaged in many regrettable activities that I am not proud of. My life involved

numerous hurdles, evident in the scars on my face that resulted from a severe head injury. This accident led to multiple stitches, leaving me in a coma for three months in the ICU.

At one critical point, the medical staff declared my survival unlikely and scheduled the removal of life support at 10:00 a.m. However, a supernatural intervention occurred when a woman walked into my room and proclaimed I would be healed as I was a man called to the nations. Miraculously, at exactly 10:00 a.m., I woke up and started to regain my strength. X-rays revealed that I had a loss of bone structure from the hip down, leaving me without feeling. However, God healed me physically, and as I walked out of the hospital, I began to pray over people for them to also be healed. I prayed for healing from cancer for one particular lady, and she was miraculously healed. She turned to me and called me Pastor—this was a significant moment for me. The spirit of boastfulness was hitting me hard, and my dad encouraged me to fast and pray. This marked the beginning of the journey into ministry.

God taught me how to pray, lay hands on the sick, and discern hidden conditions. I personally did not have the power to heal; it was a divine gift. My ministry grew, eventually leading to the establishment of our church. Presently, I serve as the senior pastor, overseeing a team of twenty-four pastors throughout Fiji.

Then Pastor Vili turned to Nate, saying, "God woke me at 4:00 a.m. this morning to begin praying for you both, and He showed me so many things—Man of God, I can see you standing behind a pulpit. I can see you with a coat, with a necktie speaking to many."

With tears cascading down my face, I marveled, as this was the exact same vision I had years ago. Pastor Vili turned to me and said,

> I can see you, ma'am, with women surrounding you, and the majority of them are kneeling on the floor. I can see vibrations coming from your hands. It's going to touch people, and when you leave this place to go out, God will do two things for both of you. One, God will ignite prophecy and hidden things in your life, and God will allow that to happen when you lay your hands on people. There is no sickness that is under the sun that will walk away from you. And likewise for you, ma'am, God is going to use your life so mightily. I see people who are dark, people who are from all walks of life—Chinese, Malaysians, Indonesians—they will come from every different walk of life. They will come to you. God will use you two so mightily in God's Kingdom.

I can see the angels in your ministry. God allowed for you to come to this nation for a man of God to give you the words of prophecy so that you can see God's call in your life for so many years. God has been touching your hearts because of your good hearts and because of every good thing that you have done for people. There is a big reward, and I can see that God is going to fulfill every dream about every account—every dream about dollar signs. When you get home, this will be accelerated. God will increase you so mightily that people will be standing on the side touching their chest and wondering how come, but what they don't realize is that this is God's power. God is revealing so many things.

He said, "Let's hold hands and pray."

Heavenly Father, we know that it is not an accident and that You reveal hidden things; Your power led us to leave our nation to come to this nation so that You will allow in such a way the words of prophecy to move into our life that you are calling us in the last days in 2022 for prosperity into our life that they will increase in multitudes in multitudes. Father, thank you so much that you are anointing them today for them to grow so rapidly. Whatever they lay their hands on, people will be healed and released from all kinds of sickness. In Jesus's mighty name, I release this anointing into their life, and may the vibrations of God start working right now from the top of their heads to the soles of their feet. Touch them and whatever they want in a mighty way. Thank you so much. Even things that they think about will come to pass; you'll move in a mighty way. Thank you for the healing, thank you for this moment. In Jesus's mighty name, we pray. Amen!

The Spirit of God filled that car and we wept. We also prayed for the pastor, asking for protection, favor, and a long life for him and his ministry. We prayed against any curses spoken against him and declared a new season of blessings. We prayed for God's angels to watch over him and raise up warriors for His Kingdom, and that his ministry would be a legacy of faith and miracles.

Nathan offered a specific prayer, during which he mentioned to Pastor Vili that he envisioned him finding favor in the Fijian government. Approximately a year later, while Pastor Vili was conversing with Nate over the phone, he revealed that earlier that morning, he had visited the prime minister's office to pray for him and the government. Wow!

After our return from Fiji, neither of us were ever the same. We saw God's providence in this entire adventure, and this trip was so much more than a bucket list vacation. We had received a call from God to fly across the world and be inconvenienced by a very timely cyclone so we could meet a couple who informed us about a driver named Dan, who had a ringtone that led us straight to Pastor Vili, who had a specific word from God that we both needed to hear and receive. Pastor Vili spoke life into and over us, setting in motion a trajectory that would forever change our lives. God is always moving; we just have to decide if we are willing to trust and move with Him.

THE GIFT

As a little girl, I knew we all had a guardian angel, and my prayers were always for mine to be the Archangel Michael himself. I figured it was because he was a powerful angel mentioned in the Bible. Though I wasn't entirely sure why his name stood out, I suppose I felt the need for a strong angel by my side. God did answer my prayer, not in the way I had imagined, but in His own unique special way.

Inspired by Pastor Vili's testimony and our yearning for what he had prophesied, we decided to embark on a forty-day fast once we arrived home from Fiji. This was also symbolic since both of us were turning forty years old.

About six months after our fast, one of Nate's employees began experiencing a persistent cough that worsened over time. A CT scan revealed the harsh reality—stage 4 small cell lung cancer. He remained determined to continue working while undergoing chemotherapy locally in order to stay close to his wife, Cindy.

Sadly, the man's first marriage dissolved after he and his wife lost two sons, one from a tragic car accident at the age of ten and the other only two years later from cancer. Now, with his own cancer diagnosis, his most pressing concern was the care of Cindy, whom he'd been married to for thirty years.

In a confidential conversation with Nate, the man revealed another layer of their story. Cindy suffered from severe agoraphobia, never leaving their home due to overwhelming fear. He took care of all errands, and they even built a ten-foot privacy fence to create a safe space for her. Cindy's avoidance of people, even close relatives, was her way of protecting herself from the harsh realities of life she'd endured.

As the man's condition worsened, Nate stepped in to support his colleague by taking him to and from chemotherapy visits. This marked the beginning of their deepening friendship. Concerned about Cindy's well-being in the event of his passing, he approached Nate with a heartfelt request to take care of Cindy to the best of Nate's abilities. Touched by the trust placed in him, Nate made the commitment to fulfill this promise.

Unbeknownst to Nate, he became the only person Cindy had ever allowed beyond their entryway. This was a significant gesture, as Cindy had never extended this level of trust to anyone other than her husband. Nate found himself navigating the intricacies of their household, discovering that Cindy was unaware of their financial status and lacked knowledge of managing bills and basic household tasks. This situation provided him with the opportunity to truly understand and support the couple during a challenging time.

But one of Nate's greatest concerns was regarding the man's spiritual well-being. So, he prayed and asked God for a clear opportunity to share the love of Jesus without being offensive or pushy.

His colleague had only attended church during holidays in his youth, and the man confided in Nate that his approach leaned toward wanting scientific proof of God's existence. What initially seemed like a challenge became a setup for Nate, as he was equipped with a deep scientific and biblical understanding of Christianity. Nate was able to specifically address each skepticism. He skillfully weaved evidence from the Bible and science to demonstrate that God does indeed exist and performs miracles today. Furthermore, our personal stories became an integral part of the discussion, making it challenging to dismiss the reality of God's presence. Our experiences served as living proof that God is real and continues to work miracles.

When Nate inquired about his friend's relationship with God, he openly admitted to feeling uncertain about where to begin. Expressing a desire to believe, he confessed that his faith was challenging and complicated. He shared that he has tried to live a good life, with the hope that his positive actions will outweigh his negative ones, ultimately securing him a place in Heaven. Nate responded, "You don't have to wait. You can know God now. It's really simple." Nate continued, "Jesus died on the cross for all your sins. He is the only way to eternal life, and all you have to do is believe and confess that he died for you and ask God to forgive you of your sins. Jesus will forgive you, and you don't have to 'hope,' but you can know you will go to Heaven when you die." The man looked at Nate deeply and responded, "I do believe in Jesus as my Savior." So, sitting in Nate's car driving to his next chemo visit, he verbally confessed that he believed in Jesus.

A short time later, in January 2022, both Cindy and the man became ill with a severe respiratory illness, which interrupted the man's first chemotherapy infusion. Cindy experienced swelling and difficulty getting up from the couch. One day, feeling unwell, she entered the restroom and shouted to her husband that she was dying. Weak from cancer, he entered with a pulse oximeter and observed Cindy's levels had dropped dangerously low, so he urgently called 911. When the paramedics arrived, they faced challenges trying to assist her in the small bathroom. Her oxygen saturation rapidly declined, and he heard them say, "Stay with us." Because of his own illness, he couldn't ride in the ambulance. A few hours later, he received a heartbreaking call from the hospital—Cindy had not made it.

Devastated by the loss of his beloved wife, the man found himself alone, reaching out to Nate and colleagues for support. Dying, with no wife, children, sister, or father, and only his elderly mother in California, he felt the weight of his situation. Now battling cancer alone, he leaned on Nate during this difficult time. However, Nate noticed that despite the recent loss of his wife and the battle with stage 4 cancer, he had a remarkable strength in his ability to persevere, not just physically but mentally. He was ready to fight with all his might for the battle that lay ahead.

In the early stages of his battle with cancer, the man enjoyed having us over to share his days. He was lonely from the loss of his wife and wanted to visit. It was during those one-on-one times I came to truly see the depth of his humor and intelligence. I would offer to clean his house, especially his dust-covered curtains or restroom, but he always insisted that I simply sit with him at the table and visit. Fortunately, my job's flexibility allowed me to spend most Wednesdays with him, listening to his stories and learning about his life. He created a welcoming atmosphere, arranging chairs for conversations and getting us our favorite coffee.

One day, as we sat across from each other, I asked, "How do you cope with so much loss?" He smiled and then shared, "Yes, I cry and get upset, but life goes on, and I have to either choose to live or not. Since I've always been a fighter, my mantra in life and with all its challenges is—'Let it go.'" As I gazed into his eyes, I saw the remnants of the scars and pain he had endured as a little boy. He had been molested by the one person meant to provide safety in his life—his father. The weight of his losses was palpable, having endured the tragic deaths of both his children, the inability to save his wife, and the passing of his father and sister.

Despite every challenge, he never succumbed to despair; he never threw in the towel. His philosophy, though simple, inspired me to keep moving forward and to find value in the progress made. His resilience and outlook left a lasting impact on me.

The man had mixed emotions about our boys, perhaps due to his own loss of sons, yet he liked it when they were near. When they visited, they were quiet, respectful, and understanding of his chemo struggles. In one beautiful and spontaneous moment, as we prepared to leave his house, Caleb expressed his desire to pray. Moved by his sincerity, I turned and asked if it would be all right for the boys to pray for him. Without hesitation, he welcomed the offer and even requested prayer for his hearing. Caleb, at just eleven years old, gently placed his hands on the man's head and began to pray. His words were filled with the sweetness and authenticity of a child. His powerful prayer resonated, "Lord, I pray for peace and that you give comfort during this time. Lord, I ask that you open his left ear, not just so he can hear, but that he would hear straight from you, Lord." It was during this sweet yet powerful prayer that each of us felt the atmosphere change. The Lord touched the man's ear; indeed, he could hear better physically, but more significantly, he could hear straight from the Lord.

He requested a Bible and began delving into the Scriptures, listening to pastors on TV, and even starting to financially support global ministries.

He told us that he's not a man of elaborate prayers, but his favorite prayer growing up had been, "God, help me and thank you." He felt ashamed telling us of his simple prayers because they were not eloquent like others, but Nate and I reassured him that God looks and sees his heart; heartfelt prayers are honored by God more than lofty ones.

Sadly, the man's cancer spread to his brain and he lost the ability to eat, causing him to lose a lot of weight. At a height of six feet two inches, he went from 225 pounds to 142 pounds. With the cancer spreading rapidly and his health failing, he could no longer receive chemotherapy. He was in denial about the reality of his situation and wanted to continue with chemotherapy or any new trial drug available.

One day, things shifted when he asked Nate for two favors: One, he did not want to die alone, and two, he wanted us to accept all that he owned because he did not want it to go to the state, and his mother was so elderly she didn't want the burden of it. Speechless and yet extremely grateful, we accepted, vowing to honor his memory. I expressed my profound gratitude and explained how this would forever change the trajectory of our lives. I vowed that someday I would write a book to tell the world about his kindness to our family.

One special moment came in his final days. I began reading him this story that I had begun writing. With tears in his eyes, he said he felt very unworthy to be included in my book, as he had made some horrendous mistakes in his past, and frankly, he felt very rough around the edges. I assured him that in the three years of knowing him, I had seen God do a miraculous change in his life, regardless of being rough around the edges. I reminded him of the thief on the cross, emphasizing that if the thief recognized Jesus as Lord, it didn't matter what his past held. What mattered in that moment was the thief's future and where he was heading—to be with Jesus in eternity!

And speaking of divine interventions, remember my prayer as a little girl when I wished for my guardian angel to be named Michael? Well, God had sent us this man, Michael MacRay. He departed his earthly home in 2023. Although Michael was not my guardian angel, he became an unexpected and transformative presence in our family, providing us with the finances to write this book in ways that only God could orchestrate. Oh, and his house was perfectly located a stone's throw away from the entrance of my childhood home, in Roanoke, Texas, Brookstone. Because Michael financially blessed us, we were then able to turn around and bless Pastor Vili's ministry in Fiji and other ministries that are growing God's Kingdom. Although Michael felt insignificant in the Kingdom of God, God used his life to profoundly impact the nations, even after his death.

Nate and I never expected a relationship with a once-random stranger to develop so quickly. I have a tendency to be reserved with others, and often find it challenging to trust people because of past experiences where relationships fell apart after becoming too close. However, when we let go of our facades, people can genuinely care for each other because we all need each other!

We are all unique, with different opinions and experiences, and that's actually a good thing. It serves as a reminder that we are all handcrafted individuals, shaped by our unique paths in life—I witnessed this truth in my relationship with Michael.

Michael told me one time, "It's a little weird knowing when you're going to die. Everyone knows that they will die eventually, but usually, it's a surprise. However, being terminal, I know it will happen sooner rather than later." Then he continued, "But that's why it's important to live each day like it's your last."

STRIVING

After our trip to Fiji, the Lord had ignited something within me, something that had long been dormant. However, much like my childhood self, I expected immediate results and grew impatient. I found myself desiring God to act on my timeline, since I wasn't getting any younger and was about to turn forty years old. Days and months passed without any visible progress, and I once again succumbed to discouragement. In an attempt to start my calling, I auditioned for the worship team at the megachurch we were now attending. I envisioned a warm welcome, believing they were eagerly anticipating my presence on their stage. To my surprise, the reality was quite the opposite. Not only was I met with a resounding no, but I was also assigned to a beginner vocal class focused on breathing, alongside my eldest son, Ethan. The experience left me humiliated, embarrassed, upset, and disappointed, as my ego took a considerable blow. I can't remember how many classes there were, but it was going to take years to "work" my way to the top-class level, and even then, there was no guarantee I would ever make it on their worship team.

Compounding matters, the introductory vocal class requested a singing recording for constructive feedback, and I did not know that declining was an option. Unfortunately, when the specific day came, I was grappling with the flu, complete with fever, stuffy ears and a sore throat. Stuffy ears alone made it challenging to hear notes accurately and sing in tune. Despite my less-than-ideal condition, I complied with the request. However, the ensuing critique was merciless; they bluntly tore apart my vocals. Once again, I encountered rejection from the church, this time based on their perception of my lack of qualifications in the vocal department.

While driving to work, our towering megachurch loomed on my right, and frustration seized me. Gripping the steering wheel, I poured out, truthfully more like yelled, my doubts to God, "Am I not growing older? Have you forgotten about me? I'm quitting;

I'll pursue becoming a nurse practitioner, and get into aesthetics, establishing my own practice. God, you supposedly called me into ministry, but I'm not seeing it. We received this word in Fiji, but where is the fulfillment in our lives? Where is Your promise?"

In the aftermath of that emotional outburst, and even amid it, I realized my aggression toward the Lord was unwarranted, and I apologized. Despite my doubts, I knew deep down that He remained present in my life, obscured only by the clouds of uncertainty. It was almost as if God responded, "Camey, are you done? If so, now I can move. When you no longer rely solely on your own strength, when you hit rock bottom and recognize that it has nothing to do with your own strength and talents, that's when you allow me to work."

The turning point arrived when I released the metaphorical rope, which symbolized my relentless efforts to achieve and surrender my future into the hands of Jesus. I needed to let go of "my goal," which may not necessarily have aligned with God's plan and was more about my personal aspirations. I needed to put a stop to allowing approval from others to dictate my worth, put an end to constant striving and fear, and relinquish the unmet expectations I had formed in my mind.

DUNAMIS

Seated in the church service, I waited as the pastor prepared to reveal the word for the year. Taking the microphone, he declared, "This is the year of dunamis."

In an instant, I had a flashback of Nate and me seated in the breakfast area in Fiji. The anticipated crystal-clear waters were replaced by a murky sight from the storm, yet the sun reflected a mesmerizing glistening. I had just asked Nate if he had a word for the year. After a thoughtful and lengthy pause, I blurted out, "My word for the year is power!"

When my mind returned to the church service, the pastor began to explain the meaning of dunamis in Greek, which is power. As he passionately preached, the resonance of the word dunamis seemed to physically vibrate through my body, and a newfound boldness washed over me—just as Pastor Vili had prophesied.

PROVIDENCE

During a conversation with a well-known evangelist, a mighty man of God whom I respect, I shared my experiences about visiting Fiji and how we were given Michael's home, recounting what the Lord was doing in my life. With tears in his eyes, he said, "Camey, wow, God is moving mightily in your life. The hand of God is over you, and there is a great call on your life. But, Camey, you just have to understand you must see God's providence in your life and know His Word in your heart." Encouraged, I asked if Nate could join our conversation, to which he warmly replied, "Absolutely, it would be my pleasure."

Nate joined us as I recapped some of our conversation when he turned and asked the man if he would pray over him. Without hesitation, he responded, "Absolutely, it would be my pleasure."

In that small room, Nate knelt down, raising his hands to the Lord, while the man of God placed his hand on Nate's head and lifted his other arm. As he began to pray, something extraordinary unfolded, something miraculous happened, addressing specific things the Lord had impressed upon Nate and me. The prayer over Nate consisted mainly of Scripture verses. The man of God then blessed Nate, expressing that he saw him with a mighty shield and a sword, fighting the dragon and overcoming. "Man of God, I bless you, and may you rise up! Whatever is in me that is good, I speak that same blessing over you as you are called to minister to men around the world. May you continue to hide God's Word in your heart and know the Lord is so pleased. Thank you, God, that Nate is being lifted up and carried on this enormous wave. To God be the glory!"

At that moment, my jaw dropped. A year earlier, Nate, who seldom has vivid dreams, recounted a dream where he found himself in the ocean surrounded by a crowd. Suddenly, an immense wave appeared, lifting him effortlessly while others struggled. Nathan surfed the wave and calmly stepped on the shore. This was truly a word from the Lord.

We hold that moment dear because that precious man of God went to meet Jesus just a few days later. I feel incredibly honored to have known Dr. Steve Farrar and his wife, Mary, and his prayers and words of encouragement have forever changed our lives.

Shortly after our visit, I began to reflect on the meaning of God's providence. The sovereignty of God reflects His caring provision for His people as He leads us on our path of faith through this life, accomplishing His purpose in us. While God is in control, I am not a robot; I have choices to make. God will use all things, the good, the bad, and the ugly, to fulfill His perfect plan, and thankfully,

God is with us through it all. Ephesians 1:11–14 says, "In him, we were also chosen, having been predestined according to the plan of Him who works out everything in conformity with the purpose of his will. So that we, who were the first to put our hope in Christ, might be for the praise of his glory. And you also were included in Christ when you heard the message of truth, the Gospel of your salvation. You were marked in Him with a seal, the promised Holy Spirit when you believed."

When I question the ways of God, I am reminded of these profound and encouraging words that Steve's wife, Mary, spoke to me. May they speak to your heart as they have to mine.

> Yes. God is holy, He is love, He is just. He is good, merciful, gracious. He is also all-powerful. He is sovereign, ruling over all of the affairs of history and men. In the case of deep scars, providence brings together goodness and suffering in a way that is glorious, and yes, beautiful. It tempts even the coldest of cynics and draws in the most crushed in spirit.

Just a month later, I found myself in the exact same room where Steve prayed for Nate and me. Another man of God, Mike, gazed deep into my eyes before I could utter a single word. He said matter-of-factly, "Your story will be a movie one day." I responded with a knowing smile, "I believe so, too, Mike . . . one day." Mike, too, left this Earth shortly after, and he joined the Army for the Lord!

PRISON MINISTRY

As a young child, I was captivated by a movie with a dramatic plot involving a woman who entered prisons to aid inmates, only to fall in love with one and assist in his escape. Despite the questionable storyline, it left a lasting impact on me, and I decided at a young age that I wanted to pursue prison ministry.

My first experience with prison ministry occurred in high school in south Texas. I participated in singing and distributing supplies at a juvenile facility and found my heart deeply moved. The experience was transformative; I felt a connection with juvenile inmates who seemed genuinely happy that we chose to visit and share. Although I didn't have another opportunity to help with a prison ministry for many years, the calling never left me.

Now, a group of individuals who, like me, had been rejected by the megachurch worship department formed our own team, focusing on an all-male inmate facility in Bridgeport. My heart ached for these men, recognizing the gravity of their decisions, yet knowing that God wanted them to surrender all of their brokenness—every broken piece. Witnessing the hand of God upon their lives was profound, as I watched many worship with a freedom that surpassed even some individuals I've seen outside prison walls.

One day, the team asked me to lead a song; fear rushed over me since I hadn't led a song in years. Yet, my mom's advice still rang clear in my mind, "Camey, get your eyes off yourself and walk in your giftings." One particular song on the list of options resonated so deeply within me, and it was a song I knew. Truthfully, I had always wanted to sing it, yet was never given an opportunity. The song was titled "What a Beautiful Name."

After several team rehearsals, the night of worship arrived, and we were standing in front of three hundred men. We also were significantly behind schedule, and an unusual sense of nervousness overcame me. As time was running short, our team leader for the evening, Mindy, spoke up and said, "Wait, we have one more song that we must do." As I began to sing "What a Beautiful Name," I could sense the atmosphere shift. When the song reached the phrase, "what a powerful name," the presence of God filled the room so strongly that I, along with others, couldn't stand and were brought to our knees in worship. I knew it was the Lord. I was grateful on that particular day that I had worn a big, flowing shawl, so people couldn't see me trembling. My arms and legs shook, not out of nervousness, but under the power of the Holy Spirit—the unmistakable dunamis, the power of the Lord moving within me. That night, I experienced something amazing when the presence of God visited that prison!

I suppose another reason I feel such a deep connection to people in prison is that, in reality, we are all prisoners of sin. The only difference is that some of us get caught, while others are con artists, able to conceal it and avoid detection. Regardless, I am reminded that God sees it all. Despite the heinous crimes some of these men are incarcerated for, God's presence in that prison serves as a powerful reminder that nothing is beyond the reach of Christ's love. The moment I begin to perceive myself as superior to anyone else, I recognize that I am becoming enslaved. I heard a preacher once say, "We are all recovering sinners prone to relapse." We all require the mercy and grace of God every day and every hour. As the old hymn reminds me, "I need Thee, Lord, I need Thee."

CHAPTER NINETEEN

Revealed

(OVERCOMING SCARS)

My scars bear witness that I have fought battles that I have overcome as the victor. I stand, not in my own strength but in His, boldly declaring my triumph over all my scars. As I've displayed throughout, I have had many internal scars. Scars of abandonment, rejection, prejudice, anger, comparison, pride, and shame. But it was the scar of abandonment, intricately woven with the thread of rejection—that feeling of being unwanted—that was a constant companion on my journey. While I always knew that my family in Guatemala loved me and did not reject me, the experience of separation and being cared for at an orphanage left an indelible mark that I never fully understood. Abandonment took root when I was left alone in a crib, and its echoes still reverberate in my psyche. I have since learned that early childhood trauma rewires the brain in an infant and they are unable to understand the long-term effects until later in life.

This adds context to my worry that kids would reject me because of my scars, my husband would choose someone else and continue to repeatedly turn to pornography, that pastors would reject me and my voice.

Trauma ignited my emotions, almost as though I were on steroids, causing me often to go straight into fight or flight mode. Choosing anger and pride, I fought with my words and justified my actions with my fear of not being heard or understood by others. My hurt was displayed through anger, which served as a defense mechanism to protect my hidden emotions. I was afraid of so many things, especially a narrative about me that did not align with the truth. I also disliked being the subject of someone's conversation when I was not present to defend myself. I would struggle to articulate my emotions effectively and become assertive; consequently, I would sometimes resort to shouting forcefully to make myself heard.

Rejection bred comparison of myself with others, but shame was the true enemy of my soul. It was definitely the loudest voice in my mind, as it condemned me to hide out of a fear of abandonment. I could not bear the rejection of others, so I held people at a distance. Shame took charge of memories and distorted them, altering my self-perception, and kept me stuck in self-disgrace. Fear of others discovering my flaws fueled constant worry about rejection.

For years, shame has tried to silence my voice. I used to question, "Who holds the keys to my shame? Who made me feel imperfect and unworthy of belonging? Who silenced my emotional expression by taking away my voice?"

> " I went back and reclaimed what was surrendered, lost, and stolen with Jesus. "

Now that I can identify my scars, I am better equipped to address the lies that are beneath them. I choose to speak into the scars rather than let them define me. My perspective has shifted, and I no longer see my scars as something to hide but opportunities to overcome.

I revisited those difficult moments and looked back into the files of the memories that were stored and locked away. But this time, I went back with Jesus, the One who holds all power overcame fear, death, and the grave. I went back and reclaimed what was surrendered, lost, and stolen with Jesus. I needed Jesus. When I turned to Him, He extended an invitation to unburden myself and to let Him redefine my scars. He taught me that I don't need to fight the battles but to trust that He is a good father who will never forsake me and will fight my battles.

However, the enemy knows my weaknesses and where to strike, and at times, it feels like I face opposition from others who constantly question my identity and acceptance.

> *Now that I can identify my scars, I am better equipped to address the lies that are beneath them. I choose to speak into the scars rather than let them define me.*

Someone who knows me well and has heard my story many times asked me, "So, Camey, what is your real name?" Taken off guard, I replied, "Camey?" "No," the person persisted, "What is your real name?"

I clarified myself, thinking he was referring to Camen, and said, "Oh, my real name is Camen."

When he emphasized the word real, I felt it was an attempt to nullify my adopted name. While my Spanish name is beautiful to me, the frustration arose from his attack on my identity. Despite my explanation, he continued to ask, "No, I'm talking about your

Spanish one, you know, your real name." Frustrated, I admitted, "My real name is Camen Joy Thompson." Did his question insinuate that my identity lay in my past as Santos Clementina, not as a true member of the Thompson family?

Suppressing my hurt, I spoke to the sabotaging spirit of rejection hidden behind their words and declared, "I've been adopted and chosen, and my name is Camen Joy Thompson!" With that, our conversation came to an end. In the divine ledger of existence, I knew I was grafted into the Thompson family, with my "blood" and DNA now intertwined with theirs. The heartbeat that once belonged solely to them had become mine, a rhythmic echo of belonging and total integration. Family transcends the limitations of genetics; it's a connection through unconditional love, acceptance, and shared experiences. My earthly adoption gave me legal rights to my new name.

In the same way, God has adopted me and given me a new name. Therefore, I choose to be identified by that new name. We gain legal authority in the Kingdom of God when we choose to submit our past to Jesus and accept His free gift of grace. He has accepted and adopted us, and no one can take away our inheritance.

> *Family transcends the limitations of genetics; it's a connection through unconditional love, acceptance, and shared experiences.*

To claim it, we just need to get to know Him. I can testify of this because I did it. I became friends with Jesus, got to know Him by reading the Bible, and understood that His love had no conditions. I had to take what I knew in my brain and tell my heart that love comes from the Creator of the Universe. Even though I am loved, I am also a broken individual in desperate need of a Savior, in need of healing and forgiveness, as we all are.

> "Even though I am loved, I am also a broken individual in desperate need of a Savior, in need of healing and forgiveness, as we all are."

So here I am, proclaiming my testimony with the King of Kings, the Commander of Angels Armies, with my sword at my side, ready to ride with others into battle, unlocking doors of freedom. I am no longer bound in the silence of shame to hide my story because there is power in my testimony, and I have been set free!

NATE AND I MOVING AS ONE

Nate and I continue to serve God (the big "C" Church), and are now better at recognizing manipulation, sooner rather than later. Over the years, we have learned the importance of walking in freedom from bitterness, anger, resentment, and lack of forgiveness. We strive to walk in joy and peace. Nate, our boys, and I find ourselves working together as one. The days of doubt and hesitation have passed.

While our marriage is far from flawless, our daily pursuit of the Lord has brought us closer together. We are committed, not just to acknowledging our individual areas for improvement but to demolish sin at its root. Setting healthy boundaries has become a valuable tool for us in not allowing sin to gain a stronghold. Our boundaries are not intended to create distance between ourselves or others; instead, the boundary serves to help us exercise self-control, determining what we will accept and will not tolerate. My spicy personality no longer threatens Nate, and now he encourages me to walk boldly and confidently in my God-given calling.

My boys are my greatest achievement, and being a mother has brought me the most joy. I wholeheartedly know that our boys are carrying the legacy of God's providence, destined to make an impact for His Kingdom on Earth. Ethan possesses an extraordinary gift from God, a natural ability to master any musical instrument, compose, sing, and lead others in worship. He has thoughts and visions of leading worship.

Caleb or Caleb Rea Rea as we call him, is a sports enthusiast and a die-hard Dallas Cowboys fan with a fierce competitive spirit, yet he also possesses a servant's heart, a pastor's heart, like my dad, Rea. It's remarkable how he even resembles my dad in many ways. This is just another miraculous example of how adoption carries DNA.

Eli, our youngest son, is the joy and laughter in our family. He's quick-witted, humorous, and a talented video gamer @EliNugz. He has a heart for evangelism as he eagerly and boldly shares his faith wherever he goes. He has even mentioned having visions of himself speaking to others about God in front of many people.

My family is the heartbeat of my life's song, orchestrating a harmonious and beautiful melody.

UNHIDDEN

Sitting here typing, reflecting on life, I realize my story has been concealed, hidden in plain sight to others. I'm reminded of Old Testament giants like Moses, hidden in a basket from Pharaoh; Gideon hiding in the winepress; Joseph hidden in Egypt from his brothers; Esther adopted and awaiting the fulfillment of her promise; and David in the field of training, despite having been anointed king. I questioned God again about why I was hidden in plain sight, but then was reminded of God's perfect providence. If this story had been revealed earlier, it would have been prematurely released, as my many chapters had not yet been written. My heart would not have been in the right place, and I would have most certainly crumbled. I had to go through preparation, in both my heart and my life, before I was ready to see the fulfillment of the promise He spoke over me. I express my gratitude to the Lord with a shout of hallelujah for His perfect timing, His ongoing protection, and His hand over my life, which safeguarded me—even from myself.

My voice was meant to be heard at this time, for you to hear of my trials, tribulations, embarrassments, failures, and sins, but also to rejoice with me how I overcame only because of the grace of God. I wouldn't trade even one of these experiences since each one has brought me to where I am today.

DELIVERANCE IN THE SCARS

Scars are a result of being wounded and serve as evidence that healing took place. They signify not just the wound but also the triumph over our adversity. When we overcome through the power of Jesus, we no longer live in shame or condemnation because our scars become a living testament, recounting our healing journey.

I want to tread very carefully here, as in no way do I intend to compare myself to the Apostle Paul. But for the sake of this story, I replaced chains with scars in this paraphrase of Philippians 1:12–18:

> What has happened to me has actually served to advance the Gospel. As a result, I have scars, but I will proclaim the Gospel without fear. I will rejoice, I will testify, because I want you to know what has happened to me. Despite all my opposition, I will testify of my scars of deliverance. I will labor and fight for His Kingdom, proclaiming the good news of Christ to nations. My testimony will advance the Gospel.

The enemy wants to take you out, destroy or hinder your progress in every way, but unknowingly, the enemy has opened up a way for your story to unfold and come forth. Because of what you have gone through, you now have the ability to see the world differently.

Years ago, my mom shared a profound insight with me:

"You know, Camey, we're all born with a cleft."

I looked at her like she was ridiculous because what she was saying simply wasn't true. She then continued, "We are all born with a cleft in our heart that separates us from God. And the only one who can heal this gaping void is the Great Physician, and His name is Jesus. He is the only one who can stitch our beautiful hearts, make us whole, and bring us to Himself."

This statement has consistently encouraged me. On days when discouragement sets in and I want to throw in the towel, my thoughts get clouded by the enemy's words. I catch myself only looking at the scars in my reflection. That's when I hear my mom's words: "Camey, don't focus on yourself; it's not all about you."

At the time she spoke those words, they felt a little harsh, but she was speaking the truth. All along, the Lord has gently shifted my focus away from my scars, to look at His scars. Friends, it is only through His beautiful scars of redemption on the cross that we can choose salvation—the scars that bring deliverance, freedom, and healing.

The sacrifice of Christ on the cross allows us to live without hiding or feeling ashamed. He gives us hope, purpose, and the chance to spend eternity with Him—how beautiful!

It is truly remarkable that after Jesus rose from the dead, He could have easily hidden or erased His scars. However, in a powerful act of love and humility, He chose to keep them as a reminder of the immense suffering and ultimate sacrifice He endured for our sake. As He stood before His disciples, He showed them His hands and side, wearing the scars as proof of His resurrection. These scars symbolize victory, as Jesus conquered death and now holds the keys to eternal life. His scars tell His story, a constant reminder of His love and sacrifice for us.

My story without God is nothing more than a mere overcoming story since many others have faced incredible challenges far more serious than mine. My story is not just a narrative of endurance. Instead, the pivotal moment that occurred when I was five while seated in the back of a car, changed my life forever. God spoke to me, revealing that He would use my scars to point to His scars.

You have to know that even with scars and imperfections, you are loved, you are chosen, and you are accepted by the Creator of the Universe. Romans 8:15 echoes the truth that we, too, have received the spirit of adoption. The reality is that we live in a fallen world that has been tainted by sin and brokenness. There is no denying it: we will fight battles, and we will be left with scars, whether they are physical, emotional, or spiritual. You are unique and special to Him and He will be with you. As you read this, I believe God wants to touch and heal the darkest places in your heart. I pray that your most difficult moments become powerful testimonies of God's goodness and grace. As you begin this healing journey, you will also hold the keys to help unlock healing in the lives of others. You carry authority.

~

It all started with God's providence in my life, saving me and transforming each beautiful scar into a narrative of His goodness. Whether these scars are external or internal, God is using them to bring healing to me, ultimately positioning me to extend healing to others. God wants to partner with you to bring you to a place of healing as well, and then for you to take your keys and unlock doors for others.

If you're simply reading my story, it's a small story. However, I exist within a much larger narrative where God is actively at work—not just in me but also in you. God is crafting a unique story in you as you are marked for a purpose—you too are beautifully scarred.

CONCLUSION

The Promise of My Name

As I stood backstage, behind the curtains, preparing to speak with those butterflies in my stomach, Nate brought up my birth name, Santos Clementina, and asked about its meaning. While we knew for a long time that "Santos" meant saint, we recently learned that "Clementina" means mercy or merciful. Nate was silent and quiet for a moment, so I asked what he was thinking. Supernaturally, with the Lord's help, he connected the dots.

"Though it might be a bit of a stretch," he began, "what's your biological father's name?"

"Jesús."

"That's right. Jesús, which means Jesus in English. Your dad, James Rea, goes by Rea (pronounced Ray), and what's Rea's name in Spanish?"

"King," I answered.

"Exactly. I just pictured Jesús carrying you, Clementina, to Rea. Your story since the very beginning told of His story. Jesus brought Mercy, because of His great love, to the King!"

With tears in both of our eyes, I spoke through happy tears,

"Nate, I was carried all along by Jesus and shown mercy to stand before the King. God knew it all along!"

And in all of His mercy and love, He is carrying you!

~

The crowd's roar brings me back to the present moment, as I'm reminded I'm here to share my story. The thunderous applause echoes throughout the arena, a symphony of gratitude directed not toward me, but toward the Lord. Taking a deep breath, I whisper a prayer, "Lord, I choose to partner with You . . . let's do this."

As I make my way onto the stage, the energy is palpable. I scan the sea of faces in the audience. My gaze falls upon those who have shaped my life: Rita and Jesús, who taught me what unconditional love looks like, sitting next to my biological siblings; my adopted siblings Shelly, Shannon, Tyler, and Piper surrounded by their spouses and families; and my dad and mom, who taught me to accept the gift of adoption. I'm honored to have had a front-row seat in the Thompson home full of love and laughter. Their cheers of never quitting are what propelled me to this moment. I also spot Dr. Hobar, Dr. Anderson-Cermin, and Dr. Byrd who gave me more than a fighting chance and championed me in my calling. God used their hands as the miracle in my life. Wilda, Marleen, Pastor Bob, Pastor Liz and Crystal, Pastor Vili from Fiji, Tarah, Stephen, and Wendy. But it is the smile from my husband Nate and our three boys that literally takes my breath away. Nate is the one who kissed my scars and showed me unconditional love and that I was worthy of being loved. My boys are my heart, the beat of my song! But God . . . this story is all about You—and I tell it for You. When people hear me sing may they know that it was You who gave me my voice. May You receive all the glory and honor, and may my life reflect Your glory pointing others back to you.

I sense the room is filled with a mighty army of angels and also those who had gone before, Michael, Steve, and Mike, giants in the faith, cheering me on. But it was the words of Wendy, spoken over me years ago, that resonate in my heart at this moment:

> The Lord is going to bring an increase of anointing on your singing and praising. I sense that if you don't already write, He's going to start using your writings, and He will show you the words that you hear because they are really powerful, and they are going to be used to set people free. He's building character and a deeper love in your heart and in the hearts of others because of the trials that you have gone through. But He likes to show you off! He wants you to know that He sees you and encourages you to release hope over you for what is coming.

MAY GOD USE MY SCARS TO POINT TO HIS SCARS!

The End

"How beautiful is the body of Christ."

How Beautiful - Twila Paris

In Loving Memory
Jesús Molina Flores
March 22, 1942 – March 29, 2024

Arrived at Spokane International Airport

Lake Shoecraft, Washington State

From left to right: Back row - Piper, Shannon, Shelly, and Tyler. Front row - Camey, Judi, Rea, and Carlos.

Camey and Dr. Hobar

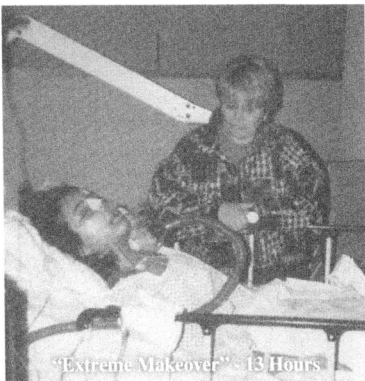
"Extreme Makeover" - 13 Hours

From left to right: Ethan, Nathan, Camey, Eli, and Caleb.
Credit - Macie Joy Photography

Letter From Nate

My wife's story is a powerful example of God's mercy and miraculous providence that saved her life. It's a beautiful story, but incomplete without telling ours. Our testimony is hard to read at times, yet without its raw portrayal, it falls short of the work God did in our lives. I firmly believe our story is not unique and is shared by countless marriages across the world. We live in a deeply broken and fallen world that is seeking wholeness and belonging. I prayed about what to share, and believe God asked us to not hide behind the pages of this book but to proclaim from the mountaintops how He set me free from the striving and lies that held me in bondage for far too long.

    I spent most of my life playing the good guy while living as a masterful liar. I was fooled into thinking I could live bound to lust secretly while publicly pretending to be a "sold-out" Christian. Many who read this may think that bondage to pornography is typical for most men in today's society. Right now, this may even be your story.

    I absolutely hate that this is part of our story, but I am so happy it's not the end. God is in the restoration business. We see time and time again how God uses the least qualified to bring the fullness of His work. My life is but a piece of this tapestry that God is weaving in all of us. It took me nineteen years stuck in bondage to fully learn what it means to live a submitted life to God. Oh, how I wish I had learned this when I was younger. That is why I now speak openly of the pitfalls of hidden sin, especially sexual sin. The shame it brings is immense and only perpetuates the vicious cycle of lies and destructive behavior.

We all are confronted with the impact of our sin at some point. However, our pride can suppress what God truly requires—complete surrender. Sacrifice is at the center of atonement, and Jesus was the ultimate and final sacrifice that releases us from the debt of sin. In turn, Jesus wants us to accept this free gift and begin the process of dying to our flesh. This requires us to die to our desires, pride, and the scars we carry.

I thank God for arresting my heart in a miraculous way that ultimately saved me and my marriage. This is also available to you right now. If you are dealing with sin and feel you will never find freedom, perhaps there needs to be a death first in order to find life.

I thank God for the day I died, so I can now live free in Christ!

Sincerely,

Nate

Letter From Dr. Hoban

LEAP Global Missions is a nonprofit organization that is dedicated to enhancing and enriching the lives of people around the world by providing free specialized medical and surgical services inspired by the love of Christ. Our medical volunteers give their time and talents free of charge to help others who are sometimes in difficult circumstances. This year, after 33 years, LEAP Global Missions surpassed 10,000 surgeries and procedures provided to people from 24 countries whose lives have been dramatically changed through surgical gifts. That is amazing in and of itself, particularly given the fact that LEAP was started out as a single mission trip to the Dominican Republic in 1991. Out of that initial endeavor, a miracle happened. We have had hundreds of medical volunteers give up income, vacation time, and the security of home to travel to different parts of the world to help people, mostly children, receive care to which they have limited or no access. God created LEAP Global Missions through that effort of many stepping forward in faith to help someone in need.

Like the amazing gift that LEAP has been, meeting and getting to know Camey and Nathan has been a tremendous gift to my wife Robin and myself. We even asked Camey to sing at our daughter's wedding! Camey's story provides a perfect example of how surgery and love can powerfully change the circumstances of a child born with a cleft.

We travel to places where surgery is not readily available to children with clefts and other craniofacial conditions. Like Camey, a child born with a cleft lip and/or cleft palate will require multiple surgeries over their development years. We always go back to make sure those patients have an opportunity to get all the care they need as they grow. We provide everything needed to care for a child with a cleft, collaborate with our international partners to improve the conditions of the facilities where we work, and seek to train local surgeons in performing specialized surgeries to make care more accessible in their countries in the future. Still, we continue to walk alongside and help those skills and self-reliance mature and blossom.

We are blessed with generous donors who have seen our dedication over 33 years and support us in our efforts. If you would like to become one of those supporters, please visit leapmissions.org.

Acknowledgments

To the reader, I extend my deepest gratitude to you for joining me on this journey by reading my story. I hope that one day we will have the opportunity to meet, and I can hear about your beautiful scars. Send me your story at cameyjoy.com/mystory.

To Sarah Wronko, who breathed life into me and initiated this endeavor, I owe immense gratitude. This book would not exist without your belief in me that I was called to write my story. I honor you.

To Nancy Armstrong, thank you for your gracious edits. I am beyond grateful to you for raising such an amazing son, whom I love and call my husband.

To Rea Thompson, I am profoundly thankful for your meticulous line edits, for ensuring my dates and timeline are accurate, for allowing me to sit and hear stories from you and Mom, and for your assistance in reducing the overuse of "that" and possessive verbs.

To Nathan Armstrong, thank you for guiding the direction and layout of this book. Your work on the book's timeline provided the kick-start and structure I needed to write. Thank you for allowing me to be transparent and honest with our story.

To my sister, Shannon Mahoney, your help in conveying the essence of my heart through the book, as well as your thoughtful editing, was invaluable. Your writing is beautiful and significant, and it truly helped convey the heart of my story. Thank you!

To my biological sister, Mirsa J. Molina, thank you for translating so I could hear part of my story from Rita and Jesús. I couldn't have done it without you.

To Katie Chambers, Beacon Point LLC, I admire your perfectionism, editing brilliance, and dedication to making my story flow seamlessly. Thank you for bringing this book to completion.

To Abby Kendall, AC Editorial, thank you for your kindness and expertise in proofreading.

To Kayla Miles, thank you for enhancing my appearance with your makeup artistry, but most of all, your friendship.

To Macie Marchand, thank you for ensuring my hair looked its best for the book cover.

To Joe Cavazos, your talent in creating an exceptional book cover is truly commendable.

To Meshali Mitchell, your creativity and zest for life are truly inspiring. Thank you for capturing my story through your camera lens.

And to the countless doctors, nurses, and staff who stood by me through every surgery—thank you from the bottom of my heart!

About The Author

Born with a bilateral cleft lip and palate in the mountains of Guatemala, Camey beat all odds and survived.

In a journey marked by sacrifice, love, and divine intervention, she underwent twenty-three surgeries in America, each one a testament to her unwavering spirit and the power of perseverance.

From the uncertainty of her early years, where doctors doubted her ability to speak clearly, to her present-day travels around the world as a speaker and singer, Camey's story is a powerful testament to the transformative power of faith and love.

She doesn't just serve God through her music and words, she also serves in her job as a nurse, touching lives with her message of hope. Because of God's love and miracles, she has a full life with her three boys—Ethan, Caleb, and Eli—and her husband, Nate. She finds immense joy in the Bible and hopes that her journey will inspire others to show their scars and find strength, healing, and freedom in their vulnerability.

CAMEYJOY.COM					FOLLOW @CAMEYJOY

Made in the USA
Coppell, TX
04 March 2026

72894924R10174